GATEWAYS
TO
TORAH

GATEWAYS TO TORAH

Joining the Ancient Conversation
on the Weekly Portion

RUSSELL RESNIK

Messianic Jewish Publishers
a division of
Messianic Jewish Communications
Baltimore, Maryland

© 2000 by Russell Resnik
All rights reserved. Published 2000.
Printed in the United States of America
Cover design by Drawing Board Studios

Back cover photo by Barbara Bray

05 04 03 02 01 00   6 5 4 3 2 1

ISBN 1-880226-88-X

Library of Congress classification number 00-133468

Lederer/Messianic Jewish Publishers
a division of
Messianic Jewish Communications
6204 Park Heights Avenue
Baltimore, Maryland 21215

Distributed by
Messianic Jewish Resources International
Individual order line: (800) 410-7367
Trade order line: (800) 733-MJRI (6574)
E-mail: lederer@MessianicJewish.net
Website: www.MessianicJewish.net

DEDICATED TO ANDREW NAGEN.
"AS IRON SHARPENS IRON . . ."

Contents

Introduction

Ben Bag Bag used to say, "Turn it, and turn it, for everything is in it. Reflect on it and grow old and gray with it. Don't turn from it, for nothing is better than it."

Pirke Avot 5.22[1]

Torah—the five books of Moses—has been a unifying force in Jewish life since the earliest days. Today virtually every synagogue in the world reads the same portion of the Torah each week, completing the cycle of readings every year. Each weekly Torah portion, called a *parasha* in Hebrew, has been the subject of commentary and discussion since before the days of Yeshua the Messiah, and continues to be today. This book is one student's contribution to the ancient discussion.

Study of the weekly parasha creates a sense of common interest with other readers, and with the Jewish community around the world and throughout the ages. In this form of study, the parasha becomes the topic of conversation. The study is more interested in considering possibilities, exploring tough questions, and discovering novel interpretations, than in reaching binding conclusions. It finds the text of Scripture to be multi-faceted, infinitely rich, and endlessly engaging. A recent book on Jewish spiritual guidance puts it this way:

> As we study sacred text—the touchstone of Jewish spirituality—we become conscious of every dimension of what is written; we also become insightfully aware of its silence. The rabbis understood this phenomenon. They drew meaning out of every aspect of the text. We should do the same.[2]

The authors encourage us to engage in the ancient conversation with and about Scripture that has been the pursuit of Jewish thinkers over the ages.

Let us consider an example of this conversation from the *Midrash*. Midrash is an entire genre of rabbinic literature that explores the meaning and implications of the text of the Hebrew Scriptures. The earliest Midrash (on Genesis) dates from the classical Amoraic period of 400–600 CE, but is based on older oral material.[3] Midrash Rabbah is the collection of such commentaries based on the five books of Moses and the five scrolls—Esther, Ruth, Song of Songs, Ecclesiastes, and Lamentations—that reached final form during the medieval period, but also reflects much older tradition.

Midrash comprises both *halacha*, or legal argument and rulings, and *haggada*, stories, homilies, and illustrations that expand the biblical text. Haggadic Midrash especially is characterized by its imaginative and creative treatment of the text. As Rabbi H. Freedman notes in his introduction to *Midrash Rabbah*, it

> . . . continued to express the ideas, aspirations, hopes, fears, and collective thoughts of the people of Israel in successive generations. Many of the thoughts in the Haggadic Midrash were due to poetic inspiration, and these were often ahead of their times. In this sense they were prophetic, and in respect of function they continued the prophetic tradition, though formally and chronologically they were the direct descendants of the Scriptures, children of their verses, souls of their soul.[4]

Midrash Rabbah on Numbers 7:19 considers the offering of "one silver bowl of seventy shekels" presented by the tribe of Issachar. This bowl, it says, represents the Torah, because Issachar was considered the tribe of great Torah scholars. Furthermore, the Midrash claims, Torah is like wine and it is customary to drink wine in a bowl, like the silver bowl of the offering. But why is the bowl seventy shekels in weight? "As the numerical value of *yayin* (wine) is seventy, so there are seventy modes of expounding the Torah."[5]

The point of this rather imaginative (even by Midrashic standards) interpretation is that Torah has multiple meanings and applications. As Ben Bag Bag says in the reference from Pirke Avot above, "Everything is in it." Moreover, it is to the Torah's glory that it has such a wealth of meanings. Seventy is a number of completion and perfection, ten times seven. It intimates that every verse of Torah is filled with meaning. The best Jewish minds throughout the ages will spend their best energies exploring its meaning and never come to the end of it. Further, says the Midrash, seventy is equivalent to *yayin*, wine, according to the Hebrew numbering system. Torah yields sweet and even intoxicating meanings as we drink of it deeply.

Thus Rashi, the great medieval Torah commentator,[6] savors the views of his predecessors, explains them, and expands upon them. He often seems just as interested in keeping the conversation going as in uncovering the one true meaning of the passage under consideration. Rashi is considered the definitive commentator. His approach to Scripture defines the Jewish outlook and methodology to this day, and it often reads like a friendly conversation.

In the same way, Ramban, another great medieval commentator,[7] comments on the opening words of the book of Leviticus or Vayikra. Vayikra begins with an unusual verbal construction, literally, "And he called to Moses, and the Lord spoke to him from the tent of meeting." Ramban explains that the Lord had to *call* to Moses because Moses would otherwise not be able to enter the tent of meeting, according to Exodus 40:35.[8] He then goes on to give a different, earlier opinion concerning the use of the word "call" in this verse.

> "All communications [that came to Moses], whether they are introduced by the word *dabeir* (speak), or by *emor* (say), or *tzav* (command), were preceded by a call," that is to say, G-d said to him, *'Moses, Moses'* and he answered, *'Here am I.'* This was a way of expressing affection and encouragement to Moses.[9]

Finally, Ramban adds a third interpretation. According to the "way of the Truth," his code phrase for *kabbala* (Jewish mysticism), the verse under consideration is like Exodus 24:1—"Now He said to Moses, 'Come up to the LORD, you and Aaron, Nadab and Abihu, and seventy of the elders of Israel, and worship from afar' (NKJV)." In this reading, says Ramban, the call summons Moses into the presence of Mattatron, the Angel of the Lord, but not "right up to the Proper Divine Name, *for man shall not see Me, and live.*"[10] The call in Leviticus reiterates this call in Exodus.

Thus, Ramban gives three different interpretations of Leviticus 1:1, and makes no effort to compare their merits or to decide between them. Rather he engages us in a conversation that spans a millennium and the entire breadth of the Mediterranean world.

This approach to study stresses the process rather than the event, reflecting the way people actually tend to make decisions today. We are faced with so many choices and possibilities that we shy away from any option that demands a hard and immediate decision. In recent years, telemarketers have learned to be non-confrontational. When a prospect declines their offer, they no longer push the issue, as in the old foot-in-the-door methodology. Instead, phone solicitors accept your refusal and leave you with their 800 number just in case you have questions later. They want their call to be part of a process instead of a definitive event.

Of course, the story of Messiah is an event that ultimately demands a response. Those who believe in the authority of the sacred text and its ability to convey God's truth to every generation may balk at some of the more imaginative interpretations. I am not, of course, advocating such a treatment of Scripture as normative in all cases. But I am advocating it as a means of entering into an ancient Jewish conversation, a conversation about the things that matter most, and potentially about the Messiah.

The conversational approach is not foreign to Scripture itself. Hebraic rather than Western, it does not seek to define one precise and correct interpretation of the text, but to mine the text for its interpretive riches. This distinction does not mean that anything goes interpretively, but it does allow the possibility of multiple meanings, a possibility that Scripture seems to endorse. Thus, for example, Scripture often conveys truth through story, which is inherently more flexible and multi-faceted than straight propositional presentation. Further, Scripture itself seems more comfortable with ambiguity than many of its modern interpreters. It is beyond the scope of this introduction to go into a detailed study, but I will suggest three examples from Yeshua's teachings.

- Yeshua portrays John the Baptist as Elijah to come, as promised in Malachi 3:23–24 (4:5–6, NKJV):

Behold, I will send you Elijah the prophet
Before the coming of the great and dreadful day of the Lord.
And he will turn
The hearts of the fathers to the children,
And the hearts of the children to their fathers,
Lest I come and strike the earth with a curse.

Yeshua intimates that this prophecy will have multiple fulfillment when he says. "And **if you are willing to receive it**, he is Elijah who is to come" (Matthew 11:14, emphasis mine). He demonstrates that this is the sense of his statement in Mark 9:11–13:

And they asked Him, saying, "Why do the scribes say that Elijah must come first?" Then He answered and told them, "Indeed, Elijah is coming first and restores all things. And how is it written concerning the Son of Man, that He must suffer many things and be treated with contempt? But I say to you that Elijah has also come, and they did to him whatever they wished, as it is written of him." (NKJV)

- In the Olivet discourse, Yeshua mentions the "'abomination of desolation' spoken of by Daniel the prophet" (Matt. 24:15, NKJV). Yeshua undoubtedly was aware of the fulfillment of this prophecy in the days of Antiochus, when the Seleucids defiled the Temple. Yet, here he seems to apply it both to the first century Roman destruction and to a final catastrophe at the end of the age. It is one original prophecy spoken by Daniel, but it has multiple meanings in its outworking through history.

- When Yeshua disputes with the Sadducees concerning the resurrection, he says, "But concerning the dead, that they rise, have you not read in the book of Moses, in the burning bush passage, how God spoke to him, saying, 'I am the God of Abraham, the God of Isaac, and the God of Jacob'? He is not the God of the dead, but the God of the living. You are therefore greatly mistaken" (Mark 12:26-27, NKJV). This is an imaginative use of Scripture that discovers new and unexpected meaning in a familiar passage, without depriving it of its more obvious meaning, much as does the Midrash.

Significantly, Mark records that "one of the scribes," an expert in the Jewish conversation concerning Torah, overheard Yeshua and "saw that he had answered them well" (12:28). Yeshua's hermeneutic approach would have gotten him drummed out of many modern seminaries, but it was highly credible in the eyes of his Jewish contemporary. It may be an approach that would further Jewish appreciation of the Scriptures today.

My method in these studies is not systematic. I do not seek to cover the entire content of each parasha.[11] Instead, I comment intensively on a key verse or passage and its message for today. I draw heavily upon the New Covenant Scriptures as the inspired development of the Torah, but I do not seek to use the Torah as an apologetic for the New Covenant or faith in Messiah. Rather, I seek to hear the message of Torah, to listen to the ancient discussion of the message, and to advance the discussion wherever it may lead. My emphasis is haggadic, not halachic, emphasizing story, illustrations, and broad principles, rather than precise questions of Jewish law. For the sake of continuity, I provide a brief overview of each of the five books of Torah before commenting on the separate portions.

You may notice several features that are common to most of my commentaries. They will often build upon a consideration of specific word usage. This is typical of Midrash and draws us into the text itself without theological presuppositions. In many cases, I provide my own literal translation of the text to preserve the original impact of the Hebrew. You can check with the various modern translations as necessary. Also, the studies engage traditional Jewish sources conversationally, not necessarily agreeing or disagreeing, but joining the discussion on their terms. The studies often project dissatisfaction with typical, modern ways of interpretation that have not delivered the spiritual goods. Finally, their tone is not didactic—the studies often point toward Messiah, but are rarely dogmatic. Rather they keep the process going. The ancient conversation continues.

I thank the members of my congregation, Adat Yeshua, Albu-querque, New Mexico, and all of my readers and fellow students of the Torah, without whom these studies would never have come into being. And I thank my wife, Jane, for her steady support, wise insights, and participation in the vision. "A woman of valor, who can find?"

בראשית
The Book of Genesis

Genesis in the Hebrew Scriptures is called B'resheet, "in the beginning." It is the account of origins—the creation of heaven and earth and the human race, God's blessing over his creation, humankind's first rebellion, and God's initial choice of Abraham and his descendants to be his covenant people.

Genesis comprises twelve portions or *parashiyot*. The first two cover the first twenty generations of man and tell the early history of the whole human race. The final ten parashiyot cover only four generations of one human family. From the cosmic grandeur of the creation account, they bring us to familiar scenes of marriage, family, human love, and misunderstanding. The initial purpose of blessing expressed at the creation becomes lodged in this one very human family.

The message of B'resheet is that the Creator of heavens and earth is the one true God, and he has revealed himself uniquely to Abraham and his descendants, the tribes of Israel. The God of Israel has a good plan for all the nations, and he will accomplish it through Israel. After recounting the first generations of Israel, the book ends on a transitional note. The twelve tribes leave the land promised to them and descend to Egypt to survive famine. Jacob dies after pronouncing a prophetic blessing upon each tribe, and eventually Joseph, whose story dominates the final quarter of Genesis, dies as well. The book ends with Israel in Egypt and Israel's destiny unfulfilled.

Translator Everett Fox identifies seven major themes that recur throughout Genesis: [1]

1. Origins.
2. Order and meaning in history. This theme is reinforced by the use of a stylized chronology and by key numbers such as 3, 7, and 40.
3. Blessing.

4. Covenant. God concludes agreements with human beings that express his purpose of blessing.
5. God punishes evildoing. God defines and upholds justice, despite human rebellion.
6. Sibling conflict, with the younger usually emerging as the victor. This demonstrates that God's choice, not natural circumstances, determines human destiny.
7. Testing. "God tests those who are to carry forth his mission; the result is the development of moral character."

It is evident through all these themes that God the creator remains intimately involved in his creation, and especially in the human story that unfolds within it.

Blessing and Boundary

Parashat B'resheet, Genesis 1:1–6:8

God by his nature remains mysterious and beyond our human categories of understanding. If we attempt to define him ourselves, we reduce his deity to our own feeble terminology. In Scripture, however, God defines himself in ways that we humans can understand. In the first parasha of the Torah God reveals himself to be, above all, the One who speaks:

> In the beginning God created the heavens and the earth. Now the earth was unformed and void, and darkness was upon the face of the deep. And the Spirit of God was hovering over the face of the waters. Then God said, "Let there be light"; and there was light. And God saw the light, that it was good; and God divided the light from the darkness. And God called the light Day, and the darkness he called Night. And there was evening and there was morning, one day.

God speaks and the world comes into being. He creates simply by his word, out of nothing. Thus, Ramban in his commentary on Genesis writes:

> The Holy One, blessed be he, created all things from absolute non-existence. . . . Now we have no expression in the sacred language for bringing forth something from nothing other than the word *Bara* [translated "created" in our text].

The Psalmist also recognizes God as the One who creates by his own word:

> By the word of the Lord
> the heavens were made,
> And all of their host
> by the breath of his mouth. (Psalm 33:6)

Likewise in the siddur (prayer book), *Pesukei d'zimrah*—The Verses of Praise—open with the statement, "Blessed is he who spoke, and the world came into being—blessed is he." All other praises of God depend on recognizing him as the One who speaks the word of creation. This creative speech is inherent to the character of God.

In God's creative speech we find a basis for our own spiritual lives. His speech toward us, if we will hear it, creates life, blessing and peace, vision and fruitfulness. Spiritual practices such as prayer, Torah study, quietness, and service help us to receive his word. They lead us toward an inward surrender by which our souls come to resemble the "the face of the deep" over which the Spirit of God hovered at the creation.

Besides speaking the creative word, God also "saw the light, that it was good." He **sees** what he has created and evaluates it. But why does God need to evaluate what he has made? If he intended to create light, it is going to come into being exactly as he intended. Furthermore, when we humans speak of goodness it is only relative. Something we create is good only in relationship to something else. To what does God compare his own creation when he says that it is good? God pronounces "It is good" to demonstrate that he not only creates the physical world, but he also creates meaning. He creates not only things, but value. We have, then, both the creative word from God and the defining word from God. We dwell in a universe that is not only material, but also ultimately moral.

God speaks these two types of word to man as well as to the universe. The creative word becomes a word of blessing, and the defining word a word of boundary.

> And God said, "Let us make man in our image, after our likeness, and let them have dominion over the fish of the sea, over the birds of the air, and over the cattle, over all

the earth and over every creeping thing that creeps on the earth." And God created man in his own image; in the image of God he created him; male and female created he them. Then God blessed them, and God said to them, "Be fruitful and multiply and fill the earth and subdue it; have dominion over the fish of the sea, over the birds of the air, and over every living thing that moves on the earth." (Gen. 1:26–28)

This blessing is creative because, like God's utterance, "Let there be light," it is spoken out of nothing. Man has done nothing to merit a blessing. Rather, God speaks it out of his own purpose and desire. Like the primal word of creation, the primal blessing arises from God's own purpose, and it produces life. Man receives this creative word of blessing at the outset of his existence, and it becomes part of his ideal spiritual nature, defining his entire relationship with his Creator.

The original blessing includes the command to subdue the earth. Work is part of the blessing. When God places humankind in the Garden, before Adam sins, God gives him the task of working the garden; he must "tend and keep it" (Gen. 2:15). The Hebrew root for tend is *avad*, from which comes the word *avodah*, meaning labor, or even bondage. Later in the Torah, this same word also comes to mean worship, as in *avodat mishkan*, the service or worship in the Tabernacle. Avodah becomes the general term in Hebrew for worship. Perhaps worship and work are not so far apart in the mind of God.

God also tells Adam to "keep" the Garden. The root verb here is *shamar*, "to guard." As with *avad*, this word takes on a spiritual significance; it becomes the word for religious observance. When the Lord tells Israel to keep the Shabbat, he uses the imperative form *sh'mor*: keep, observe, guard.

"Tend and keep" are included in the word of blessing, but God also gives a word of boundary in the garden: "Of every tree of the garden you may freely eat; but of the tree of the knowledge of good and evil you shall not eat, for in the day that you eat of it you shall surely die" (Gen. 2:16-17). God sets the boundary. He defines what is good, and does not grant this privilege to man. He creates man in his image, but retains this matter of making moral absolutes as his own domain. In the garden man represents God, but he is not to become morally autonomous by eating of the Tree of Knowledge.

When the serpent tempts the human couple and they eat of the tree, they must be expelled from the garden. But they are not expelled without a promise, implicit in God's words to the serpent:

I will put enmity
Between you and the woman,
And between your seed and her seed;
He shall bruise your head,
And you shall bruise his heel.

Adam and Eve are deceived, and humankind becomes alienated from its Creator. Nonetheless, this alienation does not eliminate the original blessing. One will come as the seed of woman to destroy the deceiver and his works. As descendants of the first couple, we remain without the Garden, but not without hope; we can trust in God's promise of redemption. Meanwhile, his blessing remains, undeserved, but shining upon us like the creative word out of the darkness, "Let there be light."

God of Two Names

Parashat Noach, Genesis 6:9–11:32

"And God said to Noah, 'The end of all flesh has come before me . . .'" (Gen. 6:13). God speaks to Noah, and to Noah alone. It hardly seems fair. Even in that distant past there must have been millions of humans upon the face of the earth, all doomed to be wiped out by a flood, and God speaks to only one. Why is this so? The text suggests that God speaks to Noah because Noah listens.

Noah, we read, "was *tamim* [complete, whole-hearted] in his generations" (6:9). The ancient commentators debate why Torah says "in his generations." Why does it not just say that he was tamim? One view sees this phrase as a praise of Noah. He lived in a wicked generation, but remained whole-hearted for God. That is why God spoke to him. The other view says, "in his generations" because Noah was only whole-hearted in comparison to the wickedness of his generation. These commentators criticize Noah: God speaks to him and tells him that a flood is coming, but Noah does nothing to rescue the people. A few generations later Abraham, in contrast, argues with God when he learns of the impending destruction of Sodom and Gomorrah. He stands in God's way to avert the judgment against the wicked. Why does Noah not do the same?

The truth, as often in Genesis, embraces both views. Noah is righteous because he stands in opposition to his evil generation, yet he could have done more to save them. Nevertheless, whether his righteousness is great or only relative, unlike the rest of his generation Noah listens to God.

Furthermore, Torah says that Noah walked with God. His listening produces behavior. He heard God, and he did what God said. When God speaks, he gives us direction; he intends to change the course of our life. Noah set an example by resisting the current of his generation, hearing from God, and walking with him. This response is pictured by the ark. Noah enters the ark and its isolation, yet even there he has a mission from God. He is not there just to protect himself, but to carry forward God's purpose, the promise of redemption God first gave in the Garden of Eden.

Our walk with God will also require times of isolation. We may need to resist our own generation, as Noah did, if we desire to be right before God. Our whole-heartedness for God may lead us into an ark, but we are not to enter it for ourselves alone. A life of worship does not find its goal in isolation, but in walking with God within the generation in which he has placed us.

So perhaps God spoke to Noah because Noah was listening, and was willing to respond. This passage is one of the few times that Torah says *Vayyomer Elohim* —"and God said"—instead of the usual *Vayyomer Adonai*—"and the Lord said." Elohim is a general term for God as Creator and Judge. The first chapter of Genesis always speaks of God as Elohim. The rabbis said that ideally God is judge. In a perfect world everything would run according to his original plan and God would sit as judge and keep it all running properly. We do not live in an ideal world, however. Because of man's fallibility, God also reveals himself as Adonai. This is a proper name, not just a common noun, the personal name that embodies God in his grace and his mercy.

In the story of Noah we first read, "And Adonai saw that the wickedness of man was great in the earth . . . and Adonai repented of having made man . . . and Noah found grace in the eyes of Adonai" (6:5–8). But then we read that "Noah walked with Elohim (6:9), the earth was corrupt before Elohim (6:11), and Elohim said to Noah . . ." (6:13) From now on in the story it is always Elohim, with a couple of significant exceptions. Adonai tells Noah to go into the ark. When Noah and his family and the animals enter the huge ark to prepare for the deluge, we read "Adonai shut him in" (7:16), giving personal attention to the safety of the refugees. After the flood Noah builds an altar to Adonai, the first altar explicitly mentioned in Scripture. Adonai, the God of grace and mercy, receives the offering from humankind. The offering is not an attempt to sway the God of justice toward us. No, the offering is an intimate act of worship and so Noah brings it to Adonai.

Noah's greatness is his ability to embrace fully both names of God. He sees Elohim the Judge in all of his righteous wrath. We hear the Flood story so often that we may forget that it was a terrible catastrophe, an apocalypse, and a judgment. God was righteous in his judgment, but for Noah it was still a terrifying event. The cries of those being destroyed in judgment came to his ears. Confined in this ark for months, he understood God as Elohim. When the flood abated and Noah came out of the ark, his first act was to build an altar to Adonai. He was able to still worship and love him despite all that he had endured.

It is a great pitfall in the spiritual life to develop an imbalanced, flattened view of God and his complexity, to reduce God to our own neat categories. Then we worship the one aspect of God that happens to appeal to us. Noah instead worshiped whole-heartedly.

At times, Torah combines the two names of God, as the Lord God or Adonai Elohim. In all the Tanach (Hebrew Bible or "Old Testament") the two names are combined 49 times. But twenty of those times, more than half, appear in Genesis chapters two and three, relating the creation and fall of humankind. Man in his ideal state is created to relate to both aspects of God. Through his sin, he fractures that relationship, and the rest of the story of Genesis tells of these two elements of God being reconciled. Or rather, it tells of the two halves of man's understanding of God being reconciled. God is not fractured, but we are, and so we develop a fractured view of God. Scripture reveals both aspects and restores them to our understanding.

What is it like if we direct our worship toward Elohim alone? It can become guilt-ridden, mechanical, lacking in joy. Even if you are confident that you line up with all the requirements, such worship remains external and superficial.

Perhaps the other extreme is more common in our generation, leaving out the Elohim aspect altogether. God becomes the Good Lord for whom anything goes. Worship becomes a matter of individual experimentation and self-expression that only cultivates our human limitation. We do not grow.

In the siddur, just before the Shema, we recite a blessing that begins "With abounding love you have loved us." In this prayer, we ask God to unite our hearts to love and to fear his name. Many thoughtful people have a hard time with this idea of the fear of God. If he is gracious and compassionate, why do we have to fear him? But he is Adonai Elohim, God of justice as well as mercy. We ask God to unite our hearts to serve him out of love, and according to the way that he has ordained. Yeshua said, "If you love me keep my commandments" (John 14:15). God defines who he is and who we are. He seeks not a do-it-yourself worship, but worship pursued in submission to him.

Tent and Altar

The Lord says to Abraham, *Lekh L'kha*, "Go for yourself, get your-self out of your homeland to the land I will show you," and Abra-ham goes. This act of simple obedience is a watershed of human history. Humankind (represented by Adam and Eve) had dis-obeyed God and been cast out of the Garden, had been nearly wiped out by the Deluge in the days of Noah, and had finally been scattered through the confusion of languages at the Tower of Ba-bel. The human race seemed bent on disobedience. Now one man, Abraham, obeys God's command, and human destiny is changed forever.

As Abraham begins his walk of obedience through the land of promise, he employs two opposite structures, the tent and the al-tar, to embody his response to God.

> Then Adonai appeared to Abram and said, "To your descen-dants I will give this land." And there he built an altar to Adonai, who had appeared to him. And he moved from there to the mountain east of Bethel, and he pitched his tent with Bethel on the west and Ai on the east; there he built an altar to Adonai and called on the name of Adonai. So Abram jour-neyed, going on still toward the Negev.. . . And he returned on his journey from the Negev as far as Bethel, to the place where his tent had been at the beginning, between Bethel and Ai, to the place of the altar which he had made there at first. And there Abram called on the name of Adonai. . . . Then Abram moved his tent, and went and dwelt by the tere-binths of Mamre, which are in Hebron, and built an altar there to Adonai. (Gen. 12:7–9; 13:3–4, 18, NKJV)

A tent is not built, but pitched. Where we read "Then Abram moved his tent," the Hebrew says simply "Abram tented." He tented when he set up his tent, and he tented when he took it down. The tent is temporary, portable, and unimpressive, but essential to Abraham's story. God gives him the land, but he only camps out on it; he is a sojourner waiting for the promise to be fulfilled. We can imagine the contrast between Abraham's extended camp-out and his life in Ur, the great city of Mesopotamia. "By faith he sojourned in the land of promise as in a foreign country, dwelling in tents . . . for he waited for the city which has foundations, whose builder and maker is God (Heb. 11:9–10).

When Abraham pitches his tent between Bethel and Ai, he calls on the name of Adonai. This is the distinctive name of the God of grace, the one who keeps covenant. Centuries later, however, God will tell Moses, "I appeared to Abraham, to Isaac, and to Jacob as El Shaddai, but by my name Adonai I was not known to them" (Exod. 6:3).

How is it that Abraham calls on the name Adonai, but does not "know" God by this name? He is familiar with the name itself, of course, but not with all that it implies about God. There is something of God that he does not experience. He possesses the promise, but never sees its fulfillment; he holds the title deed, but never gains the inheritance. Hence, he lives in tents in the land of promise. His descendants under Moses and Joshua will experience the fullness of God's redemption and will take possession of the land.

For now, Abraham has a share in the promise, but he knows that has not yet obtained it. His defining quality is his response to God's promise: "And he trusted in Adonai, and he accounted it to him as righteousness" (15:6). Abraham dwells in tents to indicate that he trusts God even as he awaits the fulfillment of the promise. He does not yet possess something permanent, but is trusting God for it.

In contrast to the tent, which is only pitched, Abraham does build something in the promised land. We read, "and he built there an altar." Although he possesses the title deed to the land, the only structure Abraham builds there is the one used in worship. The tent is directed earthward, the altar toward God; the tent is for this age, the altar for the age to come. An altar, unlike a tent, is solid and enduring. Upon it offerings are sent up to God. Abraham dwells in a tent in the land his descendants will inherit, but he has already attained a spiritual inheritance. God is with him for good, through all circumstances.

When we seek, like Abraham, to live by trust in the God of Israel, we embark on a journey like his. We may find his two structures helpful. The tent reminds us of the fleeting nature of most of our pursuits. We are not to neglect them or handle them carelessly, but we are to maintain a proper perspective on them. Torah does not propose a dualistic approach that values only life's "spiritual" aspects and denigrates all that is "earthly," but it does remind us to hold on to earthly things lightly. Home and career, the culture and causes of our day, all are worthy of our attention, work, and dedication, but like a tent they may be folded up and removed.

The altar is a permanent place in our lives that is directed toward God, the place from which we present our offering. The details of worship may change, but the essentials of worship remain at the center of our lives. We express this centrality by pursuing a consistent time and place of worship and making it a priority over "tent" concerns such as career and entertainment. We honor the abiding traditions of worship, such as the cycle of holidays, the riches of the siddur, or the weekly Torah readings, over the passing trends of modern life.

When Abraham revisits the places of his early journeys, the altars will still be there, although the tent is gone. The altar is the place to which we return on our spiritual journey. Outward circumstances—the tent—may change, but there is an essential place that abides. There we return to the proven sources that help us maintain our connection to God.

For now, we are tent-dwellers, although we have an altar. We are awaiting the fullness of redemption. The Kingdom of God is here, but not yet. We interact with our world and its concerns, political, social, cultural, but we do not become lost in them. As we **pitch** our tent, and **build** our altar, our journey may progress like Abraham's.

Arguing with God

Parashat Vayera, Genesis 18:1–22:24

In the beloved musical *Fiddler on the Roof*, Tevye the milkman argues with God—"Why did you let my horse lose his shoe just before Shabbat?" "Would it spoil your plans for the world to make me a wealthy man?" We are not scandalized by such arguing, but see it as a sign of Tevye's faith in a God who is involved in human affairs. Our father Abraham argues with God for the same reason—and thus pioneers the tradition of arguing that Tevye inherited.

Parashat Vayera, "and he appeared," tells how Adonai appeared in human form to Abraham to announce the impending birth of his son Isaac. As he departs with two other "men," Adonai tells Abraham that he is on his way to Sodom to see whether it is as wicked as reports indicate. But Abraham blocks his way. "Then the men turned away from there and went toward Sodom, but Abraham still stood before Adonai" (Gen. 18:22, NKJV).

Compare Abraham's resolute standing before God with his posture in a later story. In Genesis 22 God appears again to Abraham years after the promised son Isaac is born. He commands him to offer up Isaac upon an altar on Mount Moriah. When the time to make the offering draws near, Abraham tells the two servants accompanying him, "Stay here with the donkey. I and the lad will go yonder and worship, and we will come back to you." The word translated "worship" means literally to bow or prostrate oneself.

Abraham bows, surrendering to God's will completely even when, as in this command to offer up Isaac, God's will does not make sense. He adjusts his categories of understanding to the command of God, not vice versa, as we often attempt to do. This surrender to God is symbolized in our practice of bowing in worship to this day, as in the recitation of the Shema, Amidah, or Alenu prayers.

Adonai praises Abraham for his acceptance of the divine word: "Now I know that you fear God, since you have not withheld your son, your only son, from me." This is the only time in Scripture that God himself tells someone, "You fear God." After God says it he bestows great blessing upon Abraham.

Now, if the posture of **bowing** is so praiseworthy, how is it that Abraham takes the opposite posture when Adonai is about to turn toward Sodom? "But Abraham still **stood** before Adonai. And Abraham drew near. . ." Drawing near, according to Genesis Rabbah 49:8, can have three meanings: to draw near to do battle; to draw near to be reconciled; or to draw near to plead. Perhaps all three meanings are wrapped up in Abraham's action here. He does battle with God's intention to destroy Sodom; he seeks to be reconciled by working out his differences with God over Sodom's destiny; and he pleads with him on behalf of the city's inhabitants. Abraham **stands** before Adonai until all this is accomplished.

Contending with God is a source of Abraham's greatness. Noah, in contrast, was also warned of judgment but did not argue with God. Noah walked **with** God, we read in Genesis 6:9, but God called Abraham to walk **before** God (Gen. 17:1). The image reminds us of a child learning to walk. In his earliest years he walks side-by-side with his parent, but as he grows older and more confident, he may walk in front of the parent. Thus Abraham is more mature than Noah; he can turn and argue with God. Indeed, God seems to initiate the argument, saying, "Shall I hide from Abraham what I am doing?" (18:17) He wants to evoke a response from Abraham, to prompt him to argue, not for himself, but on behalf of those in Sodom. Abraham bows to accept God's will for himself, but he stands to argue with God's impending judgment of another.

This posture of standing before God on behalf of another may be termed intercession. Intercessory prayer should be part of our normal spiritual practice, for if our spirituality is oriented totally toward self, we are missing something vital. Abraham displays three characteristics that are essential for intercession.

First, Abraham recognizes the righteousness of God and the evil of sin. When he pleads for Sodom he does not ask God to minimize its sin. Rather, he asks that it be spared for the sake of the righteous individuals that might be found within it. He does not try to excuse sinners or to project a god devoid of ethical judgment. Until we agree with God concerning sin and righteousness there is no intercession. Those who minimize or excuse sin cannot intercede for sinners.

Second, Abraham avoids self-righteousness. This is the great snare in spiritual life. How are we to maintain a high and consistent standard without becoming arrogant? Through identifying with those for whom we intercede. We may say "We have sinned," instead of "They have sinned"; "Forgive us," instead of "Forgive them." Or, like Abraham, we may simply show a deep personal concern for those threatened with God's judgment.

When judgment comes upon Sodom it is not only for its notorious homosexuality, but even more for its lack of care for strangers. When the three men first appeared to Abraham, he displayed the most extravagant hospitality. Two of the men entered Sodom, where Lot also offered proper hospitality. The men tested him by refusing his offer of shelter and saying they would spend the night in the street. Lot passed the test by insisting that the men stay with him. When the citizens of Sodom sought to assault the men, Lot defended them, saying "They have come under the shadow of my roof" (Gen. 19:1–8).

Care for the stranger is an antidote to self-righteousness. Current religious discourse often seems to imitate political discourse in demonizing the opposition. Those who defend the standards of Torah not only condemn homosexual practices, but they sometimes show hatred toward homosexuals; they not only dispute religious trends that partake of idolatry and the occult, but they sometimes despise those who follow them. One who walks in Abraham's footsteps, however, practices broad hospitality, including a genuine concern for those who seem to be inviting God's judgment upon themselves.

Third, Abraham acts upon this concern by doing all he can to avert Sodom's judgment. He stands before Adonai to plead for mercy. The supreme example of such a posture is Messiah himself, who came to seek and to save the lost. He ate and drank with sinners. Why? Because "Those who are well have no need of a physician, but those who are sick. I did not come to call the righteous, but sinners to repentance" (Mark 2:17, NKJV).

Any faith that claims to be Messianic must seek to build a bridge to the world of unbelief. Our worship is incomplete without such an effort. This quality counters the "me-first" philosophy of our day that has invaded even our habits of worship and spiritual development, a philosophy that often labels deep concern for others as unhealthy or co-dependent. But real worship cannot be separated from such concern, and will often rise up to do something about it. True worshipers, like Abraham, bow before the Almighty, but they are also ready to stand before him when they need to.

Burial and Betrothal

Hayyei Sarah, Genesis 23:1–25:18

And after this, Abraham buried Sarah his wife in the cave of the field of Machpelah, before Mamre (that is, Hebron) in the land of Canaan. (Gen. 23:19)

Hebron: the name of this city draws us back from the days of the patriarchs to the tensions of our own time. The building over the cave of Machpelah, which remains a landmark in Hebron, dates back to the first century of the common era. After the fall of the Temple, Hebron became one of the four holy cities of Judaism along with Jerusalem, Tsfat, and Tiberias, and the site of a continuous Jewish presence ever since. Likewise, it is a holy site to the Muslims, who also honor Father Abraham. At Machpelah today, Jews and Muslims pray almost side by side.

In the midst of this illustrious history, we may forget that Machpelah was first the burial place for a **woman**. In Torah, a wife is not a chattel—though twice Abraham treats Sarah like one, saying she is his sister to protect himself. Rather, she is an honored partner, as is evident in the account of Sarah's burial.

When Sarah's story began, she seemed passive, following Abraham as he responded to God's call and acquiescing to his ruse that she was his sister. In the relationship with Hagar, she became more active, finally rising up against Hagar and Ishmael and demanding that they be cast out of Abraham's household. The demand was cruel, but it reveals Sarah's underlying insight and concern for the promise of God. God told Abraham, "Listen to her voice" (21:12) —she is aware of my purposes and watching out for your best interests. Indeed, in commenting on this incident the Midrash (Shemot

Rabbah 1:1) says that in matters of prophecy Abraham was second-ary to Sarah.

When God made Adam, he saw that it was not good for him to be alone and decided to make an *ezer k'negdo*, literally, a helper op-posite to him (Gen. 2:18). Rashi interprets this phrase, "If he is worthy she will be a helper; if he is not worthy, she will oppose him." Later, God rebuked Adam for listening to the voice of his wife, but this was because she was in the wrong. It is not whether the voice is masculine or feminine that matters, but whether it re-flects God's voice.

Sarah receives great honor in the Torah. It announces her death at the age of 127 with great solemnity and recounts in detail the purchase of her burial place, Abraham's first purchase in the land of his inheritance. The matriarch is honored for her true sub-mission. She is not passive, but takes initiative on behalf of Abra-ham and the destiny of her family. She does not suppress her own instincts and desires, but freely places them at the service of Adonai.

Torah endorses male leadership in the home, but men err greatly when they suppress or ignore the creative input of their wives. Scripture calls for covenant loyalty and mutual submission in marriage. This loyalty recognizes and actively undergirds God-given authority. But loyalty and submission are required of the one in authority, as well, who must recognize and honor the work of God in his partner. We are to learn from the matriarchs as well as the patriarchs.

Contemporary distrust of authority and obliteration of male-female roles both tend to eliminate this aspect of our lives, but learning to submit to one another is essential to spiritual develop-ment. We practice a communal rather than an individualistic spiri-tuality. If we are in a life situation where we never need to submit, we may be in the wrong place.

When Sarah dies, Abraham must replace this essential feminine element in his family by finding a bride for Isaac. Indeed, the title of this parasha, Hayyei Sarah, means, "Sarah lives." It begins with a burial, but continues through the betrothal of a new matriarch. Sarah will live on through the wife of Isaac.

To find this woman Abraham sends a servant back to his land and kindred. The servant prays that the Lord will indicate his choice by sending a young woman who will display a great willingness to serve. She must offer water not only to him, but to his ten camels as well. Isaac does not need a new servant, of course, but he does need a wife who will show initiative and energy in doing the right thing.

> And it came to pass before the servant had finished speaking that behold, Rebekah came out . . . And the servant ran towards her and said, "Let me drink, please, a little water from your jug." And she said, "Drink my lord," and quickly lowered her jug to her hand and gave him to drink. And when she had finished giving him drink she said, "Also for your camels I will draw until they have finished drinking." So she hurried and emptied her jug into the trough and ran again to the well to draw water, and she drew for all his camels. (Gen. 24:15–20)

Submission requires considerable alacrity. Rebekah moves "quickly," she "hurries" and "runs" to serve. In our last parasha, we saw Abraham standing before God in intercession and bowing in worship; now we may add the posture of running. In the words of the hymn, Yedid Nefesh: "Your servant will run like a deer, he will bow before your splendor."

When Rebekah runs home to tell her family about the servant, her brother Laban also runs to meet him. His running, however, contrasts with Rebekah's, for he runs ahead of his father, who is the appointed authority. When the servant introduces himself and his mission, "Laban and Bethuel [his father] answered and said, 'The thing proceeds from the Lord. . .'" (24:50) Rashi notes that Laban is mentioned first because "he was a wicked person and sprang up to answer before his father." True submission runs to serve, not on behalf of self, but on behalf of another.

Rebekah reveals another quality of genuine submission. When the servant asks her to return with him to marry his master's son, she goes voluntarily. Submission is never coerced, but is a free act of surrender and discipline. It will never violate one's conscience or personal responsibility. It can never make the excuse, "I was just following orders." Submission will honor proper authority as given by God, but it will also question or even oppose specific actions of the one in authority when necessary.

The story ends with the servant bringing Rebekah to Isaac. "And Isaac brought her into the tent of his mother Sarah, and he took Rebekah, and she became his wife, and he loved her. And Isaac was comforted for his mother" (24:67).

The Midrash says that the Shekhinah departed from Sarah's tent when she died, and returned with Rebekah. Hayyei Sarah—Sarah lives on through the character of Rebekah, a character of true submission. Neither woman is passive or servile. Indeed, in the next parasha we will see Rebekah, after her sons are grown, taking bold initiative to further God's purposes for her family. Like Sarah, she is a strong woman who freely places her strengths and desires at the service of another.

Isaac was consoled after his mother's death by Rebekah. Her submissive character yielded peace, fruitfulness, and fulfillment of God's purpose. To this day we bless our daughters on Erev Shabbat with the words, "May God make you as Sarah, Rebekah, Rachel, and Leah."

Jacob and Esau

Parashat Tol'dot, Genesis 25:19–28:9

And the Lord said to her, "Two nations are in your womb and two peoples shall be separated from within you; one shall be stronger than the other, and the elder shall serve the younger." (Gen. 25:23)

Jacob and Esau are opposites from birth, and are destined, even before birth, to oppose each other. Jacob, the younger, becomes Israel, father of the twelve tribes. Esau, the elder, loses his preeminence and becomes Edom, the archenemy of Israel. The Lord, through the prophet Malachi, pronounces his verdict on the two, "Jacob I have loved, but Esau I have hated."

Sha'ul in his letter to the Romans (9:10–13) takes up this stark contrast:

> When Rebekah had . . . conceived by one man, by our father Isaac—for the sons were not yet born nor had done any good or evil, that the purpose of God according to his own choice might stand, not of deeds, but of him who calls—it was said to her, "The elder shall serve the younger." As it is written, "Jacob I have loved, but Esau I have hated."

The sharp distinction between Jacob and Esau seems based upon nothing within them or their individual life stories, but only upon a predetermined destiny.

The rabbinic literature likewise portrays Jacob and Esau in black-and-white contrast. Esau is the embodiment of evil. From him comes the Amalek, whose enmity Israel is to remember forever until he is utterly destroyed (Deut. 25:17–19). From the Amalekites, in turn, comes Haman, the greatest enemy of the Jewish people since

Pharaoh. And Haman foreshadows the one whom the rabbis saw as the final heir of Esau, Rome. Commenting on the oracle, "Two nations are in your womb," Genesis Rabbah (63:7) says,

> There are two proud nations in your womb, each taking pride in his world, and each in his kingdom. There are two rulers of nations in your womb, Hadrian of the Gentiles and Solomon of Israel. Another interpretation: Two [peoples] hated by the nations are in your womb: all heathens hate Esau [that is imperial Rome], and all heathens hate Israel.

Hadrian was one of the greatest Roman emperors, but the Jewish people remember him as the one who crushed the Bar Kochba revolt, leveled Jerusalem, and cruelly suppressed the survivors. He is the opposite of Solomon, just as his spiritual ancestor Esau is the opposite of Jacob. Torah, however, is more even-handed toward Jacob and Esau; neither one is altogether bad or good.

Early in the story, Torah describes Jacob as an *ish tam*, a "complete" or "mild" man, a man dwelling in tents, in contrast with Esau, who is a man knowing the hunt, a man of the field (25:27). When Jacob offers to sell a bowl of lentil stew to the hungry Esau in exchange for his birthright as the firstborn, Esau readily agrees. We might be inclined to view Jacob as taking advantage of his brother, but the verdict of Torah is, "Thus Esau despised his birthright" (25:34).

Later, however, the righteous Jacob goes along with his mother Rebekah's scheme to defraud Esau of his father's blessing. Despite mitigating factors, it is clear that Jacob shares the guilt of gaining Isaac's blessing by trickery. When Esau returns to discover his loss, the Torah portrays him with tenderness and sympathy: "And Esau said to his father, 'Have you only one blessing my father? Bless me, me also, O my father!' And Esau lifted up his voice and wept" (27:38, NKJV).

Jacob flees his homeland to escape the wrath of Esau, and serves Laban, who is craftier than he, for many years. He finally returns to the land of Canaan with wives and children—and a greater sense of humility in God's presence. Yet, when Jacob encounters his brother again, Esau seems noble and forgiving, nobler than he.

What then do we say? Is there no difference between the two brothers except for God's arbitrary choice? Is that choice so thoroughly God's prerogative that it never influences how the brothers live or think? No, there is one clear difference between the two that we can trace through the whole story. Jacob values what God values and Esau does not. Jacob understands what is truly important, although he does not always understand how to obtain it. Esau, who is not altogether evil, does altogether miss the priorities of God.

Thus Esau sells his birthright because he has no concept of its worth. The birthright will make him the heir of what is for now only promised. To Esau the promise is meaningless; to Jacob it is invaluable. God's choice is not arbitrary, but reflects the choices that Esau and Jacob make.

> Pursue peace with all, and holiness, without which no one will see the Lord, keeping watch lest anyone fall short of the grace of God . . . lest there be any fornicator or godless person like Esau, who for one morsel of food sold his birthright. (Heb. 12:14–16)

Esau falls short of the grace of God because it is unimportant to him. Jacob, in contrast, recognizes the value of the promise. In this he takes after his mother Rebekah, who also recognizes what is genuinely valuable. To her the prophecy had come, "The elder will serve the younger," and she does what she believes she must to ensure that it comes true. We may not commend the way she or Jacob pursue what is important, but somehow their actions turn out to be in line with God's ultimate purposes.

Rome and Israel. The destiny of the two opposing forces in the world is shaped by a simple choice, the answer to the question, What is genuinely important? Our destiny before God is also shaped by our simple recognition of what is most important in life.

Jacob can be greedy and calculating, but he is greedy for what counts, and this is the source of his greatness. Torah does not promote moral relativity, but it does portray life realistically. God responds not only to the saintly and morally pure, but also to those who put him first. These he will purify, just as he will purify Jacob by the hand of Laban during his years of exile.

Two Stones for Jacob

Vayetze: Jacob departs Beersheba and his family's encampment in difficult circumstances. He is fleeing for his life from the wrath of his brother Esau, whom he greatly wronged. His father sends him out empty-handed and charges him to find a bride for himself—usually a costly proposition.

Jacob's journey begins in the midst of struggle and will carry him to more struggles. Indeed, he will spend most of his adult life struggling, and therefore of the three patriarchs is perhaps the one most like us. Jacob has two early encounters that will guide him in his struggles, both symbolized by a stone. These encounters provide a lesson for all that are starting out on a spiritual journey; for ourselves, our children, and those we spiritually mentor.

Jacob will spend his first night out "in a certain place" where he sleeps on the ground and has nowhere to rest his head except one of the stones of the place. That night Jacob dreamed, "and behold, a ladder was set up on the earth, and its top reached to heaven; and there the angels of God were ascending and descending on it" (28:12, NKJV).

The dream of the ladder to heaven is one of the most memorable and mysterious in Scripture. As the dream ends, the LORD confirms his covenant with Jacob, but we might wonder why he sends the dream at all. Did not God confirm the covenant with Abraham and Isaac without a dream? And what is the meaning of the ladder? As striking as it is, there has been great disagreement over its significance.

An ambiguity in the original Hebrew account of this dream provides an essential clue. The phrase, "the angels of God were ascending and descending on it" could just as correctly be rendered, "the angels of God were ascending and descending on *him*." One early Targum, or paraphrase, of this passage (Targum Neophyti) explains that the angels use the ladder to descend and gaze upon the righteous Jacob.

Jacob, however, must flee because he has defrauded his brother. He has been sent out empty-handed because he has deceived his father. Why then does he attract the admiration of angels? Jacob has received the blessing of Abraham from his father Isaac, "and indeed he shall be blessed," as Isaac declared (27:33). The angels descend on Jacob because he carries the blessing of Abraham, and the eternal plan of God is now resting upon him.

Another paraphrase of the story confirms this interpretation. Nathanael, one of the first disciples of Yeshua the Messiah, expresses amazement at his great acts of power. Yeshua responds, "You will see greater things than these. . . . Most assuredly, I say to you, hereafter you shall see heaven open, and the angels of God ascending and descending upon the Son of Man" (John 1:50–51, NKJV). The angels descend to gaze upon Yeshua because the eternal purpose of God now rests on him. Further, just as the ladder in Jacob's dream connects heaven and earth, so Yeshua himself now connects heaven and earth. He is the ladder upon which the angels ascend and descend.

When Jacob awakes from his dream, he says, "Surely the LORD is in this place, and I did not know it. . . . How awesome is this place! This is none other than the house of God, and this is the gate of heaven!" (28:16–17, NKJV) Then he takes the stone upon which he had rested his head, and sets it up as a pillar to mark the place of his encounter with God.

The original Hebrew text repeats the word *makom*, "place," several times, to draw our attention to the place of encounter with God. In this place, Jacob has come to the end of his own resources. He is guilty and empty-handed, and possesses nothing but the promise of God. This is the place of encounter with God, an encounter that depends not upon our resources or qualifications, but only upon God's blessing.

The stone that Jacob raises up signifies his discovery of God, but is also a reminder of his poverty—it was his pillow before it became his pillar! Likewise, Yeshua, who is himself our place of encounter with God, continually reminds us that we must come to an end of ourselves to find God. "For the kingdom of heaven is like treasure hidden in a field, which a man found and hid; and for joy over it he goes and sells all that he has and buys that field. For the kingdom of heaven is like a merchant seeking beautiful pearls, who, when he had found one pearl of great price, went and sold all that he had and bought it" (Matt. 13:44–46, NKJV).

We may want to begin our spiritual journey, or to send our children forth on theirs, with abundant resources, but this is not always the way things begin. In our lives, and in the lives of our children, there comes a time when we are truly on our own, when we deal with the consequences of our behavior without the help of human intervention. Then we learn to lean fully on God.

We might compare Jacob's journey, which involves his quest for a bride, with Isaac's quest for a bride. Isaac had already passed through testing at the Akedah (binding, in Gen. 22), and simply received the bride whom God provided. Jacob is untested; he still must suffer the consequences of his deception. God has been watching over him all along and will continue to do so. Only now in his poverty and need can Jacob begin to appreciate this truth. After Jacob raises the stone as his pillar to God, he can depart from the Land in confidence; he leaves his parents' tents to enter his own spiritual journey.

Jacob's second encounter comes upon his arrival in Haran and involves a second stone. This stone is large and covers the mouth of a well. Jacob rolls the stone away from the well for Rachel, whom he first meets there. She turns out to be the bride whom Jacob has been seeking.

If the pillar signifies departure and discovery, the well signifies return and remembrance. Jacob's mother Rebekah was discovered at a well. Abraham his grandfather was a well digger. Isaac spent his life keeping open the wells of Abraham. At the well, Jacob returns to the people from whom his mother came and retraces the steps of his forefathers. His encounter with God requires a return as well as a departure.

When Jacob by himself rolls away the large stone to open the well, he reveals a vital aspect of his character. He can be a conniver and a schemer, but his more prominent characteristic is zeal for the things of God. He recognizes the value of the birthright and pushes aside obstacles to get it. Like father Isaac he is an opener of wells, recognizing the great value of the proven and ancient resources, and zealous to maintain them.

Two encounters; two stones. One stone becomes the pillar that marks the place of encounter with God, and the limits of our own resources. The other stone protects the well, the proven sources of spiritual life and the example of those who went before us. The journey requires both encounters, both departure and return.

The Man of Peniel

Parashat Vayishlach, Genesis 32:4–36:43

Jacob returns to the land of Canaan from his exile in Padan Aram, but first he must wrestle a "man" who appears to him alone at night. Jacob wrestles until daybreak and finally extracts a blessing from the man, but only after he dislocates Jacob's hip joint. As the sun rises, Jacob limps away from the scene of his wrestling match to meet his brother Esau and reenter the promised land.

When Jacob asks this man his name he refuses to give it, but Rashi cites "our rabbis of blessed memory" who explained that the man was the ministering angel of Esau. Every nation has such a ministering angel or "prince" as they are termed in the book of Daniel. When Daniel attempted to intercede for Israel, his prayers were held up for three weeks by the "prince of Persia," an angelic being who fought with "Michael, one of the chief princes" as he sought to respond to Daniel's prayers. Esau is the ancestor of a multitude of nations that oppose Israel, culminating in the Roman Empire that sent Israel into its millennia-long exile. Some of the commentators, therefore, see the man—Esau's ministering angel—as Satan himself. This wrestling match is Satan's effort to thwart God's eternal purpose by preventing Jacob from returning to the promised land.

Jacob's relationship to the land has cosmic significance. When he was about to depart, Jacob dreamt of a ladder to heaven with the angels of God ascending and descending on it. He named the place of this vision Bethel, the House of God. When he was about to return to the land, he saw angels coming to escort him in (Gen. 32:2; cf. Rashi) and named the place Mahanaim, "A pair of camps"—one camp of men and one of angels. Finally, Jacob returns to Bethel where God appears to him again for the first time in twenty years and confirms his promise of the land.

Within this cosmic setting, we should not be surprised if Satan himself appears as the opposition. The Stone Chumash (p. 175) depicts the wrestling match as a struggle "between good and evil, between man's capacity to perfect himself and Satan's determination to destroy him spiritually." When Jacob prevails, the man tells him that he will no longer be called Jacob, but Israel, "for you have striven with God and with men and you have overcome" (32:29). *Elohim*, translated as "God" here, can also mean a divine being or angel. When Jacob finally meets his brother Esau, he says, "I have seen your face as one sees the face of Elohim." Rabbi Hama says that by Elohim Jacob is referring to the one he wrestled, Esau's angel (Genesis Rabbah 77:3). Esau's face resembles the face of his ministering angel whom Jacob had met the night before.

Jacob's own assessment of his encounter, however, seems to disagree with this one. He names the place of the wrestling match Peniel, the face of God, "for I have seen God face to face yet my life was spared" (Gen. 32:31). Centuries later, the prophet Hosea comments on Jacob's life, "He took his brother by the heel in the womb, and by his strength he struggled with God. Yes, he struggled with an angel and prevailed, he wept and made supplication to him. He found him at Bethel and there he spoke with us." (Hosea 12:5). True, Elohim (which appears both in the Genesis and the Hosea passage) can be translated as "divine being" or "angel," but normally it means simply "God." Jacob's exclamation that he has seen Elohim face to face and lived makes less sense if Elohim is an angel and not God himself. Finally, the same one he wrestles, according to Hosea, is the one he finds at Bethel, where God appears to Jacob to confirm his promises.

In short, Jacob believes that he has wrestled with the Lord himself. Ever eager for the blessing, he sees his own strength and cunning as the only way to get it. The Lord is the one who imparts the blessing and promises a new name to Jacob, but only after wounding him. He can only leave Peniel and enter the promised land limping. Despite this injury, however, the Torah says that Jacob arrived in Shechem shortly thereafter *shalem*, whole, intact, at peace (Gen. 33:18). Rashi says this means that he was cured of his limp. But it may be that the touch of God that seemed to hinder or wound Jacob left him shalem, **more** whole than before. The Elohim he wrestled only appeared to be Satan, the adversary, but was really God equipping him for his true destiny.

As always in the stories of Genesis, the experiences of the Fathers are lessons for the children. Our encounters sometimes have the same quality as Jacob's. We cannot tell if it is God or the adversary blocking our way. How often in our history as a people, from the time of Purim and Chanukah to the current century, have events that appeared demonic hidden a divine purpose? How often have we prevailed, not by understanding fully, but simply by holding on until daybreak?

After Shechem, Jacob finally returns to Bethel where God renames him Israel as the man had foretold, and says, "I am El Shaddai. . . . The land which I gave to Abraham and Isaac I give to you; and to your descendants after you I give this land" (Gen. 35:11–12).

At the time of the Exodus, God will tell Moses that El Shaddai is the name by which he appeared to the Patriarchs (Exod. 6:2). They knew the name YHWH, or Adonai, but it is as El Shaddai that God made a covenant with them. Hence the name appears once in the story of Abraham, when God makes the covenant of circumcision with him (Gen. 17:1); once in Isaac's life, when he imparts the blessing of Abraham to Jacob, establishing him as heir of the covenant (Gen. 28:3); and now here. The name El Shaddai will appear a final time in Genesis 48:3 when Jacob recounts his story to Joseph, and imparts the name to a new generation. This is the distinctive name of God known to the Patriarchs and passed on from father to son through four generations.

El Shaddai means God the All Sufficient, a translation based not on modern etymology, but on the sound of the words, *El she'dai*, "God who is enough." Jacob is weak and impaired, but God is sufficient. Indeed, Jacob understands God's sufficiency more fully when he is impaired. From the Patriarchs we learn a spirituality not of triumph or success, but of dependency on an all-sufficient God.

Jacob does not prevail because he figures out whom he is wrestling, but because he hangs on until daybreak. Our spiritual search is sometimes sidetracked by our effort to analyze what God is doing and why, by our attempts to define the indefinable. Sometimes the point simply is to hold on. The God we serve is ever mysterious, but he is El Shaddai, the All-Sufficient one.

The Chosen Son

Parashat Vayeshev, Genesis 37:1–40:23

The story of Joseph, which dominates the final chapters of Genesis, is also the story of Judah. Joseph is the favorite of his father, and his brothers plot to murder him out of envy. The eldest brother, Reuben, wants to save Joseph but proves ineffectual. Judah quickly emerges as the real leader and devises a scheme that does indeed save Joseph's life; the brothers sell him into slavery in Egypt. Judah is hardly upright at this point, but he spares Joseph, and unconsciously cooperates with God's purpose in the whole affair.

Before revealing what will happen to Joseph in Egypt, however, the Torah continues the story of Judah. Like his sister Dinah who earlier "went out to see the daughters of the land" (34:1), Judah "went down from his brothers" (38:1) to marry the daughter of a Canaanite.

When Dinah went out, she encountered a great tragedy. Shechem, prince of the region, "saw her; he took her, lay with her, and violated her" (34:2). Dinah's vengeful brothers Simeon and Levi eventually kill Shechem for his transgression, along with all his men.

The Midrash blames Dinah for contributing to this tragedy by going out from the shelter of her family (Genesis Rabbah 80:1–5). Does this view perpetuate the age-old male view of rape, blaming the victim for inciting the attack? After all, it seems to say, if Dinah had simply stayed home, none of this would have happened. Further, the Midrash says, Dinah is called "the daughter of Leah," because Leah also went out in a way deemed inappropriate. "When Jacob came from the field in the evening, Leah **went out** to meet him and said, 'It is to me that you must come for I have clearly hired you with my son's mandrakes (*dudaim*—an aphrodisiac root).' So he lay with her that night" (30:16). Daughter follows mother in her immodest behavior.

Jacob, however, does not blame Dinah at all; instead, he rebukes Simeon and Levi for their excessive response. Even at the end of his life, Jacob remembers their violence, curses their rage, and refuses them a full share in the inheritance of the twelve tribes.

Dinah's story revisits the dominant theme of the lives of the Patriarchs, the question of the heir. The inheritance of the spiritual legacy of Abraham cannot be determined strictly by birth order. Reuben, Jacob's first-born, had already become disqualified as leader of the sons of Israel when he went in to his father's concubine Bilhah and lay with her (35:22). Now Simeon and Levi, the second and third sons, are also disqualified. The stage is set for Judah to rise to preeminence among his brothers, but he almost misses his opportunity when he too goes off from his brothers.

In our day of extreme individualism, it is easy to forget the importance of community. God may call us one by one. We may only be able to enter his Kingdom singly, but once there, we need to recognize how dependent we are upon each other. As Dinah learned, and Judah is about to learn, we are not designed to go it alone. Instead, we receive strength through the brothers and sisters who stand with us. We need to be careful how we go out from them.

After Judah goes out from his family to marry, he fathers three sons. The oldest son takes a wife named Tamar, but dies because of his evil. The second son, according to the custom of the time, marries Tamar in order to raise up offspring for his brother, but he refuses to fulfill this responsibility and likewise dies because of his evil. Judah withholds his youngest son, Shelah, from Tamar because he is afraid that he also will die.

Eventually, Judah's wife dies. After the mourning period, Judah goes to oversee the shearing of his flocks. Tamar disguises herself as a harlot and induces Judah to lie with her, agreeing on the price of a kid from his flock. Since Judah cannot pay at the time, he gives his signet, cord, and staff as a **pledge** (*arabon*) in place of the kid to Tamar, whom he still does not recognize. Tamar becomes pregnant from this liaison and is discovered. Judah, unaware of his involvement, orders her to be executed, but Tamar produces the signet, cord, and staff, saying "By the man to whom these belong, I am with child" (38:25). Judah acknowledges that the pledge is his, and that he had wronged Tamar by withholding his son Shelah from her.

Judah is true to his pledge, coming forward publicly to redeem it at the cost of his own reputation. He even declares that Tamar is righteous, and he is in the wrong. When her time is fulfilled, Tamar gives birth to twins, Perez and Zerah. Perez will become the ancestor of King David.

Later, Judah and nine of his brothers go down to Egypt to buy food during a famine. Joseph has been elevated from slavery to become the viceroy of Egypt, in charge of food distribution. His brothers do not recognize him, but he demands that they bring the youngest brother, Benjamin, next time they come for food. Jacob, however, hesitates to let his youngest son go to Egypt until Judah steps forward: *anochi e'arvenu*, "I will pledge myself for him" (43:9). Jacob accepts Judah's offer and sends his sons, including Benjamin, back to Egypt.

Unlike the unstable Reuben, or the vengeful Simeon and Levi, Judah has shown that he will keep his pledge, even at personal expense. The brothers again stand before Joseph and he tests them by arresting Benjamin as a spy. At this crucial point Judah comes forward to offer himself in exchange for Benjamin to guarantee his freedom. This is the turning point of the story. The brothers who were willing to sell one of their own into bondage are now ready— through their representative Judah— to sell themselves into bondage to free one of their brothers.

Joseph will save the tribes of Israel from famine and bring them to safety in Egypt. But Judah gains the preeminence and becomes the ancestor of Messiah. In his final days, Jacob declares that Judah will rule over his brothers, and the scepter will not pass from him until Shiloh comes (49:10). Shiloh "alludes to the royal Messiah" according to Genesis Rabbah 98:8. In a talmudic discussion, the school of Rabbi Shila answers the question, "What is the Messiah's name?" "His name is Shiloh, for it is written, 'until Shiloh comes'" (Sanhedrin 98b).

Joseph saves his brothers. Judah, who offers himself in exchange for his brother, becomes the royal line of Israel and ancestor of Shiloh, King Messiah himself.

The Teller of Dreams

Parashat Mikketz, Genesis 41:1–44:17

Mikketz—at the end of two full years it came to pass that Pharaoh dreamed and behold, he was standing by the River. And behold, out of the River emerged seven cows, of beautiful appearance and sleek flesh, grazing in the marshland. Then behold, seven other cows emerged after them out of the River, of ugly appearance and gaunt flesh, and they stood next to the cows on the bank of the River. The ugly and gaunt cows consumed the seven beautiful and sleek cows and Pharaoh awoke. (41:1–4)

Joseph's story advances through dreams, or rather pairs of dreams, that bring about his downfall and later redemption. First, Joseph dreams that he and his brothers are binding sheaves of grain in the field, and his brothers' sheaves bow down to his sheaf. In a second dream, he sees the sun and moon and eleven stars bowing down to him. He foolishly recounts this pair of dreams to his brothers, arousing their envy and hatred. They soon sell him off to Egypt as a slave.

Years later, in a dungeon in Egypt, two fellow prisoners—formerly ministers of Pharaoh—tell Joseph their dreams, which he accurately interprets: one minister will be executed and the other restored to his office. When Pharaoh has a troubling pair of dreams two years later, the minister who was restored tells him about Joseph. He is raised up out of the dungeon and brought before Pharaoh to interpret the two-fold dream.

Solomon says that a dream comes through much concern (Eccl. 5:2). Pharaoh's concern is for his realm, and the Nile that gives it life. When Joseph is called to interpret, he does so according to

Pharaoh's concerns; he sees that Pharaoh's dreams give direction for the future of his kingdom. The dreams warn of a coming crisis and provide a basis for state policy to survive it.

We moderns, under the influence of Freud, see dreams in a similar way, but with a vastly different emphasis. Yes, a dream comes through much concern, but our real concerns, we imagine, lie in the subconscious workings of our own minds. During waking hours, our ego defenses protect the conscious mind from painful or unacceptable thoughts and desires. But during sleep the dream can penetrate our defenses and bring these repressed concerns to the surface, albeit in the veiled language of symbols so that they are not too disturbing to us. Freud saw all our concerns as linked ultimately to sexual drives and identity. Pharaoh's vision of the river might represent his own potency; the lean cows devouring the fat his fear of inadequacy or decline. Through the dream, his hidden fears and desires could find expression.

In Joseph's story, dreams are also the means of expressing what is hidden or inaccessible, but with a crucial difference. It is not the subconscious, but God who is speaking. In such a case, our ego defenses protect us from what is threatening in the nature of God. During waking hours we seek to limit God to what we think makes sense. Sometimes God employs the language of symbols, not to overcome psychological repression, but to reveal the new and unexpected to us. Through the prophet Joel the Lord speaks of the day when

> I will pour out my spirit on all flesh;
> Your sons and your daughters shall prophesy,
> Your old men shall dream dreams,
> Your young men shall see visions. (2:28, NKJV)

The dream conceals even as it reveals. It must smuggle into consciousness truth that our waking minds would ban. The dream is a gift that frees us from the analytical and man-centered mindset we would prefer. It grants us truth that we do not deserve.

Hence, it seems odd that God speaks to Pharaoh in this way. After all, he is an idolater with no concept of the God of Israel. Indeed the Midrash portrays Pharaoh as unrighteous, even by the standards of the heathen, translating "he stood by the River [i.e., the Nile, revered as a deity in Egypt]" as "he stood over the River" (which is grammatically possible in the Hebrew):

> The wicked stand over their gods, as it says, "That Pharaoh dreamed; and behold he stood over the River." But as for the righteous, their God stands over them, as it says, "And, behold, the Lord stood over him" (Gen. 28:13). (Genesis Rabbah 89.4)

In other words, Pharaoh not only worships idols, but also vaunts himself arrogantly against them. How is it that God chooses to speak to him? We might ask the same question of the young Joseph. He, unlike Pharaoh, knows God, but uses the dream of his mastery to foolishly vaunt himself over his brothers. Does God send dreams even to the arrogant and immature?

God can be generous with dreams because they do not reveal completely—someone must still interpret. The interpreter helps the dreamer gain a proper perspective. To the young Joseph his pair of dreams was so obvious that he let them speak for themselves, to his own downfall. The older Joseph interpreted the meaning of the pair of dreams of his fellow prisoners, but still failed to provide direction or comfort. One of his fellow prisoners was restored, but the other was led off to his death without a word of hope.

After this episode of interpretation Joseph must languish in prison another two years before he is brought out to interpret Pharaoh's dreams. Now at last he brings not only the interpretation, but also advice on how to respond to God's message. Dreams cannot be handled roughly. It is not enough to analyze and chart God's ways. With the interpretation must come a word of comfort, direction, or hope. It is the advice as well as the interpretation that wins for Joseph his promotion to royal status: "So the word [or the thing, the whole matter] was good in the eyes of Pharaoh and in the eyes of all his servants. And Pharaoh said to his servants, 'Can we find another like him, a man in whom is the spirit of God?'" (Gen. 41:37–38)

Centuries after Joseph, another teller of dreams arises, the prophet Daniel. When his king, Nebuchadnezzar, has a dream that speaks of his own demise, Daniel is properly solicitous. He prefaces his interpretation with the words, "May the dream concern those who hate you, and its interpretation concern your enemies!" (Dan. 4:19) He suggests to the king a course of action that may avert the foretold disaster. As with Joseph, the pagan king sees that Daniel possesses the spirit of God, a spirit that brings hope as well as wisdom (Dan. 5:11–14).

Daniel understood what Joseph finally learned. God sends not only the dream, but also the interpreter. It is not enough to interpret the ways of God, even if we have such ability. We are called also to help those for whom we interpret to respond to God's ways.

The Brothers Restored

Joseph interprets the dreams of Pharaoh and is given a position of great power in Egypt. After seven years of plenty, famine arrives and the Egyptians must come to Joseph for food. When they run out of money, he supplies food in exchange for their livestock (47:16–17). The next year the Egyptians return to buy food with nothing "but our bodies and our lands" (47:18), so Joseph provides food in exchange for land. He thereby gains all of Egypt for his master Pharaoh. To make it clear that Pharaoh now possesses all, Joseph relocates the Egyptians and requires henceforth that they return a fifth of every harvest to Pharaoh.

Joseph saves lives, as he set out to do from the day he interpreted Pharaoh's dreams, but his policy seems harsh and greedy. He reduces the starving Egyptians to slavery before he will feed them. Joseph, the man of dreams, the saint who remains faithful to God through years of oppression, seems to become an oppressor himself.

There is irony here, as we see Egypt enslaved to a son of Israel long before the sons of Israel become enslaved to Egypt. But the irony will turn on Joseph. He has given the house of Pharaoh dominion over all who dwell in Egypt. In the end a Pharaoh will arise who will use the dominion that Joseph has gained for him to enslave the Israelites.

Rashi sees Joseph's resettling of the Egyptians as a virtuous act, because he "intended thereby to remove the shame from his brothers, that the Egyptians should not call them 'exiles.'" Since all the Egyptians are uprooted, they cannot shame the uprooted Israelites in their midst. Joseph protects the reputation of his own people by humbling the Egyptians beforehand. Nevertheless, after Joseph dies the Israelites will become subject to a bondage greater than that imposed on the Egyptians. Virtuous or not, Joseph's action on behalf of Pharaoh is eventually turned against his people.

To understand Joseph's policy we must remember what drives him throughout his story—to advance the cause of the one in authority. Joseph is always the loyal second, first to his father Jacob, then to Potiphar, to the prison warden, and finally to Pharaoh. He advances in life by making the interests of the master his own. He is the ideal servant who, with no thought for himself, looks out for the affairs of the master, investing himself without reservation.

This motivation, good in itself, can lead to an unthinking devotion to the master. At the beginning of the story, Joseph curried his father's favor with little thought to his effect on his brothers. Here, toward the end of the story, he pursues the material interests of Pharaoh with little thought to the human needs of Pharaoh's subjects. Like his father, Joseph suffers from a single-minded intensity. He has the right motivation but seems to carry it too far. He thinks only of the interests of the one over him.

Joseph's single-minded intensity may help us understand his testing of his brothers. Our parasha opens with Judah's offer to become Joseph's slave in exchange for the imprisoned Benjamin. Only when he sees this display of family loyalty does Joseph reveal himself to his brothers. They have passed the test that Joseph designed for them and can now be fully restored.

The test seems to center on Benjamin, but the real issue is the brothers' treatment of their father Jacob. They sinned against their brother, but even more grievously against their father. When they sold Joseph into slavery twenty years earlier, Jacob suffered the most. Now Joseph, ever the loyal servant, is more concerned with Jacob's suffering than his own. Will his brothers do all they can to prevent Jacob from suffering this time around? Only if they do so is Joseph willing to forgive them and help them become restored.

This motivation explains another incongruity in the story. How can Joseph refrain from revealing himself to his brothers, and thereby to his father, the moment they appear in Egypt? How can he take the time for his elaborate test of the brothers when he knows his father is an old man who may not have long to live, who may die in the famine if the brothers do not respond properly?

Joseph's test undoubtedly inflicts more suffering upon his father, who sees his other sons, and especially Benjamin, threatened during the course of the trial. But for Joseph everything hinges on testing the brothers' loyalty to their father. The interests of his father come before his own; his desire to be reunited with his brothers must wait until the test is complete. Only if the brothers prove their loyalty to their father can they be restored to Joseph. The benefits of a genuine restoration, based on truth, outweigh the short-term suffering Jacob—and Joseph—must endure.

Finally the brothers' loyalty becomes clear and "Joseph could not restrain himself in the presence of all who stood before him. . . . And Joseph said to his brothers, 'I am Joseph. Is my father still alive?'" (45:1, 3) Joseph sees that his brothers have corrected their relationship to their father while he is still alive. Now his relationship with them can be restored. Repeatedly he assures them of his forgiveness.

Forgiveness is a great virtue. Messiah teaches us to practice unconditional forgiveness because we have been forgiven unconditionally. "Then Peter came to Him and said, 'Lord, how often shall my brother sin against me, and I forgive him? Up to seven times?' Yeshua said to him, 'I do not say to you, up to seven times, but up to seventy times seven'" (Matt. 18:21–22, NKJV). Still, forgiveness without restoration can become shallow or inauthentic. Yeshua forgives, but demands a change of behavior.

Joseph may have been ready to forgive his brothers as soon as he saw them, but restoration demanded that he hold them accountable for their past behavior. He will not forgive if they are still wronging their father. This demand was not easy on Joseph. At three points in the process of testing his brothers, he breaks into weeping, until finally he can no longer restrain himself in their presence.

After the death of Jacob, Joseph's brothers come to him seeking forgiveness again. With their father gone, perhaps Joseph will finally seek revenge. But Joseph weeps again and says to his brothers, "Do not be afraid, for am I in the place of God? But as for you, you meant evil against me; but God meant it for good, in order to bring it about as it is this day, to save many people alive" (50:19–20, NKJV). Joseph has defended his father's interests. He has tested his brothers' loyalty. Now he can offer them restoration as well as forgiveness.

Until Shiloh Comes

Parashat Vayechi, Genesis 47:28–50:26

Toward the end of his days, Israel who had been Jacob the heel-grabber, Israel who struggled with God, became Israel the prophet. From his deathbed, Israel spoke words of blessing over his twelve sons that foretold the destiny of their tribes far into the future. "Gather together and I will tell you what will befall you in *acharit hayamim*, the end of days" (49:1). The simple vocabulary and cadence of the Genesis narrative give way here to the more complex and difficult usage of prophecy as Jacob gazes into the distant future.

Ramban says that the phrase *acharit hayamim* describes "the days of the Messiah, for Jacob alludes to him in his words, even as he said, *Until Shiloh comes, and to him shall be the obedience of the peoples.*" This word to Judah has received the most attention of all of Jacob's final blessings, and become the subject of a millennia-long controversy:

> The scepter shall not depart from Judah,
> Nor the ruler's staff from between his feet,
> Until Shiloh comes,
> And to him shall be the obedience of the peoples. (49:10)

"Until Shiloh comes" is a literal reading of the Hebrew, but it is controversial because the word Shiloh, apparently a proper name, has not appeared in Torah before this point. It provides no clue to its own meaning. Further, as we shall see, this literal reading has received a messianic interpretation from earliest times, and thus became unacceptable to some translators.

Some translations, therefore, take Shiloh as the town of that name, which was a prominent place of worship. Here the tabernacle was set up shortly after the conquest of Canaan, and here it remained at least until the days of Samuel. These translations read, "The scepter shall not depart . . . as long as men come to Shiloh," or ". . . until he comes to Shiloh." This reading, however, would still introduce the name Shiloh out of thin air. Furthermore, it does not make sense prophetically. What special connection did the tribe of Judah have with Shiloh? The preeminence of Judah only became apparent *after* Shiloh ceased to be prominent.

Accordingly, another common tack in translation is to interpret the word *Shiloh* as *shelo*, seeing the vowel marks in the Masoretic text as slightly inaccurate. This interpretation yields, ". . . until that which is his shall come," which makes sense, but demands that we modify the authoritative Jewish text and assume a very unusual grammatical usage.

Others translate, ". . . so that tribute will come to him," or ". . . until they bring him tribute." Rashi connects the idea of tribute with a Midrashic interpretation that sees the word *Shiloh* as *shay lo*, meaning "presents [or gifts] to him," as in Psalm 76:12: "Let them bring *shay lo*, presents to him who is to be feared." But again we are tampering with the authorized text, and not really solving the problem of interpretation. It is best to let *Shiloh* stand.

"Until Shiloh comes . . ." remains the likeliest and best-attested translation. Rashi and Ramban cite it as the primary translation, as does Genesis Rabbah centuries earlier.

It is not so strange that Shiloh appears out of nowhere in the story, for this sort of thing is common in the Genesis narratives. The serpent, subtler than any beast of the field, appears without introduction to tempt Eve and Adam. Melchizedek appears without genealogy or context to bless Abraham after the rescue of Lot. A "man" appears in the night to wrestle with Jacob before he reenters the promised land. These encounters signal an event of great revelation.

Here what is revealed is the promise of Messiah, as Genesis Rabbah states "This phrase alludes to the royal Messiah" (Genesis Rabbah 98.8). Rashi says Shiloh is "Messiah the king, for the kingdom is his (SHELO)." He goes on to cite Onkelos, who paraphrased the Torah in the Aramaic language years before the appearance of Yeshua the Messiah. Onkelos also interprets *Shiloh* as Messiah. Finally, the Talmud refers to this same phrase to answer the question, "What is the Messiah's name?—The school of R.

Shila said: His name is Shiloh, for it is written, *until Shiloh come*" (Sanhedrin 98b). The emphasis on Messiah was not introduced by the followers of Yeshua the Messiah, but was seen in the text from the earliest times.

At the end of this parasha, the book of Genesis will conclude on a note of hope. The final word is "in Egypt." Why is this a hopeful ending? Because Joseph is not buried in Egypt, but placed in a coffin there. He has already taken an oath of the children of Israel, saying, "God will surely remember you, and you shall carry up my bones from here" (50:25). Joseph's coffin assures Israel that their sojourn in Egypt will not be permanent. His true burial place remains the Land promised to Abraham, Isaac, and Jacob, and the tribes of Israel will surely carry him back there. "Thus concludes the book B'resheet . . . It tells of what has occurred and of new things that will occur even before they spring up in the hearts of the people" (Ramban).

Likewise, Shiloh provides a note of hope at the end of Genesis, a hope that has already informed the entire Genesis narrative. When God cast Adam and Eve out of the garden, he told them that a "seed" of the woman would crush the head of the serpent (3:15). Noah prophesied that God would dwell in the tents of his son Shem (9:27). Abraham is promised "seed" through whom all the families of the earth would be blessed (22:18)—a promise reconfirmed to Isaac and Jacob.

The promise of the one to come is now passed on to the line of Judah. As with the Patriarchs, the promise includes a blessing to all the nations of humankind. God told Abraham that in his seed all the families of the earth would be blessed. Jacob prophesies that to Shiloh "shall be the obedience [or the gathering] of the peoples." Genesis is concerned not only with Israel, but also with all humanity, and it provides hope for all. The promise of a universal Messiah is not a late addition to Judaism, but is rooted in Torah, the vehicle of divine revelation from the beginning.

So, as Parashat Vayechi opens, the last of the patriarchs is about to die. He pronounces his final blessings in Egypt, where his people are only sojourners, but he sees hope in the future, in *acharit hayamim*, the end of days. A descendant of Judah will come before the tribe loses its preeminence. He will be called Shiloh, the one who brings Shalom—peace, wholeness, and restoration—to the children of Israel and through them to all peoples.

שׁמוֹת
The Book of Exodus

Exodus in Hebrew is the book of *Sh'mot*, or names. It opens with the names of the sons of Israel who descended to Egypt following Joseph, and quickly moves on to portray their bondage under Pharaoh. Exodus introduces Moses, who will dominate the rest of the Torah. He is the deliverer of Israel, the judge, teacher, and giver of the Torah.

Moses is most strongly connected in the popular imagination with the departure from Egypt and the giving of the tablets of law at Mount Sinai. The book of Exodus, however, spends as much time recounting the details of the law, and especially the building of the tabernacle of worship. This emphasis reflects the theme of the entire book. God sends Moses to tell Pharaoh, "Let my people go, that they might serve me" (Exod. 8:1). "Let my people go" is the theme that dominates the first half of the book; "that they might serve me" dominates the second. This service is embodied in the building of the tabernacle as the meeting place between Israel and the Lord.

Like Genesis, Exodus is also a book of origins. Abraham and his descendants have already been chosen and given the covenant promise, but it is in Exodus that God redeems them and gives them the identity and instructions that will form them as a people down to this day. Exodus also tells the origin of Torah, the instruction of God to Israel, which will dominate and become the name of the rest of the Five Books of Moses.

Along with origins, Exodus continues some other themes of the book of Genesis, such as order in history, blessing, covenant, and divine justice. It also contributes some new themes that will sound throughout the rest of Scripture:

1. Service. Will Israel serve Pharaoh or the Lord? In Exodus the word for service comes to mean worship. Exodus is the account of a struggle between the idolatrous Pharaoh and the true God for the worship of Israel.

2. Glory. At several high points in the story, the children of Israel see the glory of God, and the book concludes with an unparalleled display of glory. Even in the plagues of Egypt, God is glorified as his power is made known and displayed for humankind to see.
3. Law. The covenant made with Abraham will now be embodied in a more detailed instruction in the service of God. This instruction is passed down to all the future generations of Israelites.

As in Genesis, God is active throughout this account. Exodus carries forward the story of Israel and God's universal purposes through Israel, but above all it portrays more of the nature of the Creator, who now reveals himself as the redeemer and lawgiver of Israel.

Moshe and the Serpent

Parashat Sh'mot, Exodus 1:1–6:1

Exodus, like Genesis, is a book of creation. In Genesis, at the climax of the six days of creation, God creates humankind. In Exodus God creates a new humanity, Israel, to be his chosen people among all the peoples of the earth. In Genesis God promises the patriarchs that he will make of them a great people, but he does not fulfill the promise until Exodus.

At the opening of Genesis, God blesses humankind: "be fruitful and multiply and fill the land" (Gen. 1:28). At the opening of Exodus "the children of Israel were fruitful and increased abundantly, multiplied and became very numerous; and the land was filled with them" (Exod. 1:7). After he creates man, and at two other key points of creation, God looks upon his handiwork and sees *ki tov*, "that it is good." In Exodus, a baby boy is born and his mother sees *ki tov hu*, "that he is good" (2:2).

As the Genesis story unfolds, humankind is threatened with destruction in the waters of a flood. God commands one man, Noah, to build an ark of gopher wood, *tevat atzey gopher*, to carry him through the waters and preserve life. In Exodus, Pharaoh seeks to destroy the new humanity, Israel, by ordering his people to cast all newborn Hebrew males into the waters of the river Nile. One baby is placed in an ark of wicker, *tevat gomeh*, which carries him through the waters and preserves his life.

The daughter of Pharaoh rescues the baby and names him Moshe—"He-Who-Pulls-Out; she said: For out of the water *meshitihu*/I-pulled-him" (2:10; The Schocken Bible). Significantly, Moshe is the active participle of the root verb *mashah*, meaning to pull or draw out. Pharaoh's daughter meant to show that Moshe had been pulled out of water, but unintentionally prophesied that he would be the one to pull out others; He-Who-Pulls-Out.

When Moshe becomes a man, he makes a premature attempt to pull his people out of bondage and fails. He must flee Egypt for his life. Years later in the wilderness of Midian, the Lord reveals himself to Moshe in a burning bush and commissions him to return to Egypt and deliver his people. Moshe, older and wiser after his early attempt to be the liberator, balks at this assignment. To assure him that divine power will be with him, the Lord asks,

> "What is that in your hand?" He said, "A rod." And He said, "Cast it on the ground." So he cast it on the ground, and it became a serpent; and Moses fled from it. Then the Lord said to Moses, "Reach out your hand and take it by the tail" (and he reached out his hand and caught it, and it became a rod in his hand), "that they may believe that the Lord . . . has appeared to you" (4:3–5, NKJV).

The serpent is another reminder of the Genesis narrative, where a serpent appears in the Garden of Eden to tempt Adam and Eve. This is the "serpent of old, called the devil and Satan, who deceives the whole world" (Rev. 12:9). A rabbinic story remarkably makes a similar connection:

> A Roman lady once boasted to R. Jose: 'My God is greater than yours.' 'In which way?' he asked. She replied: 'For when your God revealed Himself unto Moses at the thorn-bush, he merely hid his face, but when he beheld the serpent, who is my god, immediately he fled from before it.' To which he replied: 'Woe to her. When our God revealed Himself at the thorn-bush, there was no room for him to flee anywhere. . . . Whereas your god, the serpent, a man can escape from merely by running away a few paces . . .' (Exodus Rabbah 3:12)

As the god of the Romans, the serpent is the god of this world, the power behind the earthly powers and kingdoms. Moshe initially flees from it in fear, but the Lord instructs him to grasp it by the tail. In the creation of a new humanity, Israel's representative must master the serpent that led the old humanity astray. For Israel

to arise as a new people out of the bondage of Egypt, the more ancient bondage of satanic deception and control must be broken.
Israel emerges from the control of the false gods. The story of the
Exodus will become a climactic contest between the God of Israel
and the demonic forces that dominate and empower Egypt.

Moshe, under the authority of the God of Israel, takes mastery
over the serpent: this encounter foreshadows Moshe's entire experience in Egypt. When he returns to the land of captivity to pull his
people out of bondage, he will not only confront Pharaoh and his
court, but also the gods of Egypt. Moshe, joined by his brother
Aharon, appears before Pharaoh to demand Israel's freedom. Pharaoh demands a sign of their authority and Moshe commands
Aharon to cast down the staff. It becomes a serpent before their
eyes. The wise men and sorcerers of Egypt, however, do the same
with their staffs through their magic arts. But the staff of Aharon
swallows up the staffs of the magicians (7:8–12). This encounter is
only the first round in a contest that culminates in ten plagues, in
which the God of Israel defeats all the of gods of Egypt—the Nile,
the sun, the House of Pharaoh.

Redemption, the theme of Exodus, is like a second creation
that restores and improves upon the first. God creates all peoples,
but in redemption he calls forth a chosen people for himself. The
redemption story—deliverance from bondage into an exalted covenant relationship with God—becomes the central story of the entire biblical narrative. It is the central paradigm for the Jewish
people, who will recount the Exodus in the yearly cycle of festivals,
in the weekly Shabbat, in prayers, and in traditions from then on.
Exodus, redemption from Egyptian bondage and elevation into
favored status with God, becomes the paradigm for the life and
work of Messiah as well.

In our times, Exodus has become the model for secular redemption, movements of liberation and national restoration in the
modern world. The original story, however, deals not only with the
hopes and struggles of a people, but with an unseen struggle between God and the spiritual forces that oppose him. Redemption is
not only freedom from bondage, it is a restoration to God that
entails the defeat of demonic forces. The serpent is put back in its
place. When Moshe pulls out his people from bondage, it is not
just a great national victory, but the restoration of divine order on
a cosmic scale.

God Makes Himself Known

Parashat Va'era, Exodus 6:2–9:35

> God spoke to Moses and said to him, *"I am
> Adonai. I appeared to Abraham, Isaac, and Jacob as
> El Shaddai, but by my name Adonai I did not make
> myself known to them."* (Exod. 6:2)

At his first encounter with God, Moshe inquires of his name and
the Lord replies, "*ehyeh asher ehyeh*—I am what I am" or "I will
be what I will be" (Exod. 3:14, NKJV). The God of Israel is beyond naming; rather he is the source of all names. He names everything that exists, but none of his creatures, including man,
may name him.

Naming implies mastery. When God created humankind, he
gave him dominion over the earth and the animals within it. In
the garden of Eden, God brought the animals to Adam to see
what he would name them, "and whatever Adam called each living creature, that was its name" (Gen. 2:19). This ability to name
reflected Adam's nature as made in the image of God. But to
name deity is beyond the powers of any human being. God will
be what he will be.

Nevertheless, God does assign himself a name by which the
Hebrews may know him:

> Thus you shall say to the children of Israel, "I AM has sent
> me to you." Moreover, God said to Moses, "Thus you shall
> say to the children of Israel: 'Adonai God of your fathers,
> the God of Abraham, the God of Isaac, and the God of
> Jacob, has sent me to you. This is my name forever, and this
> is my memorial to all generations.'" (Exod. 3:14–15)

Adonai is the name we use to pronounce the unpronounceable name of God, Yod Hay Vav Hay יהוה. Even as we employ this name, we admit that it remains mysterious and exalted, and in no way implies that we have succeeded in labeling the divine.

The Septuagint and the Hellenistic Jewish philosopher Philo paraphrase this name of God as "the One who is," the One who is eternal and self-existent, who causes all things to exist, but himself has no cause. Exodus Rabbah (3:6) notes that God says *ehyeh*—"I am" (or "I will be")—three times when he reveals himself to Moses. This shows that Adonai is the God of past, present, and future. "R. Isaac said: God said to Moses: 'Tell them that I **am** now what I always **was** and always **will be** . . .'"

The eternal and unchanging God mercifully supplies a name for himself so that human beings may call upon him, refer to him, and grow in the knowledge of him. He is Adonai, but the fathers, Abraham, Isaac, and Jacob knew him only as El Shaddai, God the all-sufficient. At first glance, it seems the LORD is saying that the fathers did not know the name Adonai, yet when we review the accounts in Genesis we see that they used this name repeatedly.

This apparent discrepancy in Exodus 6:3 became the basis for the "documentary hypothesis" of the nineteenth century, the theory that the Torah is made up of a number of different original documents. These documents used different names of God and were eventually patched together by editors who let the various names stand and did not harmonize their usage. Thus, Moses, or the editor of Exodus, is unfamiliar with Genesis, or (depending on the theory) writing before Genesis was written. He believes he is introducing the name Adonai for the first time.

There is an explanation of Exodus 6:3 that is at once simpler and more profound. The fathers were familiar with the name Adonai, but God did not make himself **known** to them by that name. That is, he did not yet reveal all the aspects of deity that the name describes. This revelation awaits the time of the Exodus. The fathers knew God as all sufficient, guiding them in their journeys and meeting all their needs, promising them offspring, blessing, and a land. Only in Exodus, however, does God invade human history to fulfill these promises.

This explanation expands our understanding of the phrase "to know God." The fathers called God Adonai, but they **knew** him only as El Shaddai. Apparently, to know God involves more than merely knowing a name for God. To know him means to directly experience his nature and activity.

The book of Exodus makes this same distinction. After generations of bondage, "God heard [Israel's] groaning, and God remembered his covenant with Abraham, Isaac, and Jacob. And God looked upon the children of Israel, and God knew" (2:24–25). God knows everything at all times, of course, but somehow he came to **know** the plight of Israel in a more direct, intense way, a way that moved him to action. To know is to incorporate something or someone into one's life so that one's own behavior is changed.

Accordingly, when Moses first approaches him, Pharaoh says, "I do not know Adonai, nor will I let the Israelites go" (5:2). Repeatedly thereafter, the Lord says that the Egyptians will come to know that he is Adonai, the one true God (7:5, 17; 8:10, 22; 9:14, 29; 14:4, 18). The Egyptians have already learned the name Adonai, but God makes himself known by sending the plagues upon them, displaying his superiority over all their false gods, and bringing out the Israelites from under the dominion of Pharaoh.

Likewise, the children of Israel will also come to know Adonai through experiencing his deliverance. Not only does Adonai enter human history and make himself known through his deeds, but he reveals by his deeds that he is the God of redemption. After telling Moses his name Adonai, he says,

> Therefore say to the children of Israel,
> I am ADONAI,
> I will bring you out from under the burdens of the Egyptians,
> I will rescue you from their bondage,
> and I will redeem you with an outstretched arm and with great
>   judgments.
> I will take you as my people and I will be your God.
> Then you shall know that I am ADONAI your God who brings
> you out from under the burden of the Egyptians.
> (Exod. 6:6–7, NKJV)

This, of course, is the great four-fold promise of redemption that provides the framework for the entire haggadah of Passover. Each cup of the Passover meal represents one of these promises. As the haggadah unfolds the story over the four cups of wine, it reveals the fullness of the redemption that Adonai accomplished for us. He is the God who redeems, who visits human beings in their need and lifts them to a position of favor in his sight. The fathers knew God deeply, but did not experience his redemption because they had not experienced bondage. Without it, their knowledge of God remained incomplete.

God is unknowable in his own nature, beyond our human categories. In our very act of defining him, we miss him, because we thereby limit his nature. But God in his mercy has defined himself. He has made himself known most of all as the merciful redeemer who delivers us from bondage. Without the experience of redemption, our knowledge of God remains incomplete.

Redemption of the Firstborn

Parashat Bo, Exodus 10:1–13:16

America's extended debate over the ethics of abortion, assisted suicide, and capital punishment has become even thornier in recent years with the development of cloning—possibly including human cloning. All of these questions concern the meaning and value of human life, and all rest upon a simpler and more profound issue: Who, or what, is the source of life?

This question stirs up the other questions: How do we define human life? Who is responsible to make this definition? To whom does a life belong, and what value are we to place upon it? Much of the controversy is in reality a struggle for final authority over human life. Who will possess it, God or human institutions?

This week's parasha reflects a similar struggle. The first Passover is the culmination of a long battle between Adonai and Pharaoh for the possession of the Israelites. To whom do the Israelites belong? What value is to be placed on their lives?

Pharaoh sought not only to keep Israel in bondage, but also to possess Israel, to take authority over the very lives of the Israelites, deciding who would live and who would die. At the beginning of the Exodus story God, the true source of life, caused Israel to thrive and multiply in Egypt. Pharaoh sought to overturn this blessing by casting the newborn Israelite males into the river, thereby usurping the authority to give life. God, in response, must make it clear that the Israelites belong to him. He commands Pharaoh to let them go: "Israel is my son, my firstborn. So I say to you, let my son go that he may serve me. But if you refuse to let him go, indeed, I will kill your son, your firstborn" (4:22–23).

Pharaoh, of course, resists this order, but the time for redemption finally comes, when Adonai makes good on his threat to kill the firstborn of Egypt. To Adonai belongs all life, not only the Israelites, but even the Egyptians. He will demonstrate this sovereignty by taking a life from each Egyptian household. To protect the Israelite households from this, the final plague, Adonai tells them to mark their doorways with the blood of a lamb.

God has already shown that he is well able to distinguish between Israel and Egypt. In the preceding plague, darkness covered all the land of Egypt, "but all the children of Israel had light in their dwellings" (10:4). At the fifth plague, Moses said, "God will make a difference between the livestock of Israel and the livestock of Egypt" (9:4). At the seventh plague, which concludes the preceding parasha, hail fell upon all the land of Egypt, except Goshen, where the Israelites lived (9:26). God needs no mark to tell him who the Israelites are.

Why, then, does Adonai require Israel to mark their doorways with blood? One line of interpretation says that the Israelites had sunken to an abysmal spiritual level in Egypt, and God provided mitzvot so they could begin to work their way back up. The mitzvah of the blood was especially potent because it required Israel to kill a lamb, which represented one of the gods of Egypt. Earlier, Pharaoh had refused to let Israel leave Egypt, but offered to allow them to sacrifice to God within the land of Egypt (8:22). Moses replied that the Israelites would sacrifice "the abomination of Egypt," which the early commentators understood as sacrificing a god of Egypt. Moses said, "If we sacrifice the abomination of the Egyptians before their eyes, then will they not stone us?" (8:23).

Ramban comments further,

> The reason for this commandment is that the constellation of Aries (the Ram) is at the height of its power in the month of Nisan. . . . Therefore, He commanded us to slaughter the sheep and to eat it in order to inform us that it was not by the power of the constellation that we went out from Egypt, but by decree of the Supreme One. And according to the opinion of our Rabbis that the Egyptians worshipped it as a deity, He has all the more informed us through this that He subdued their gods and their powers at the height of their ascendancy. And thus the Rabbis have said: *"Take you lambs and slaughter* the gods of Egypt."

Through the sacrifice, the Israelites demonstrate that they fear God more than they fear the Egyptians. Such obedience, according to this view, merits the deliverance of Passover night.

But the blood marking the doors of the Israelites signifies much more than obedience. It involves substitution. In place of the life of the firstborn that God was requiring of each household in Egypt, he would accept the life of the lamb. Substitution defines some of the most powerful scenes of Torah. At the Akedah, the Lord provides a ram as a sacrifice in place of Isaac (Gen. 22:13). At Yom Kippur, the live goat, in place of the people, carries all the sins of Israel off into the wilderness (Lev. 16:20–22). At the first Passover, God declares that all life is his—that he, not Pharaoh, has the right to the firstborn. But God will permit a substitute to be offered in place of the firstborn of Israel.

The ordinance of the firstborn, which immediately follows the account of the first Passover, builds on this truth. Adonai says, "Consecrate to me all the firstborn, whatever opens the womb among the children of Israel, both man and beast: it is mine" (13:1–2). The firstborn belongs to the Lord because it is a substitute for the whole, and God is the source of all life. God had told Pharaoh; "Israel is my firstborn." Israel as firstborn of the nations signifies that all the nations belong to the Lord.

Israel is required to redeem or buy back the firstborn because it belongs to God. This mitzvah is still observed today as *pidyon haben*, redemption of the firstborn son, thirty days after his birth. Israel, as God's firstborn, must also be redeemed out of the bondage of Egypt. The root word *padah* appears earlier at the fourth plague, when Adonai tells Pharaoh, "I will place a ransom (*p'dut*) between my people and your people" (8:19). Through redemption, the payment of a ransom, God distinguishes between Israel and Egypt. Israel has always belonged to God, but now that possession is confirmed.

What happens to the firstborn that is not redeemed? In the case of a firstborn donkey, "if you will not redeem it, then you shall break its neck. And all the firstborn of man among your sons you shall redeem" (Exod. 13:13). God chooses not to redeem the firstborn of Egypt, but to slay them, thereby demonstrating that Egypt belongs not to Pharaoh, nor to the gods of Egypt (12:12), but to the Lord, just as Israel does. The Lord takes the firstborn of Egypt, but the Israelites he redeems through the blood of the lamb.

God, the author of life, is sovereign over all life, and gives human life its immeasurable value. Pharaoh, who usurps the authority to possess and define life, ends by losing his hold on life altogether. He had sought to be lord over life, not only by holding the lives of the firstborn Israel in bondage, but also by seeking to eliminate them through infanticide. Now he will taste of death.

When we deny God's ownership of life, we diminish the value of all life, and invite violence and brutality within our gates. In all of our controversy about the definition and value of human life, we would do well not to forget this underlying truth.

He Has Become My Salvation

Parashat B'shallach, Exodus 13:17–17:16

The Hebrew Scriptures comprise three major sections—Torah, Prophets, and Holy Writings—that form one great book, the Tanach. The Tanach is a unified whole, but only one verse appears in all three of its sections, a verse from Parashat B'shallach:

> The LORD is my strength and my song,
> And he has become my salvation. (Exod. 15:2)

This couplet appears again in the Prophets, at Isaiah 12:2, and in the Holy Writings, at Psalm 118:14. The three-fold repetition underlines the importance of this verse. What does it convey that is so essential to the entire message of the Tanach?

Its first appearance comes at the climax of the Exodus story. After Israel crosses the Sea of Reeds on dry land, its waters return to drown the pursuing armies of Egypt. Adonai has gained the final victory over Pharaoh. The Israelites look upon this great miracle and lift up their voices in a song:

> I will sing unto the LORD for he has triumphed gloriously
> The horse and its rider he has thrown into the sea!
> The LORD is my strength and my song,
> And he has become my salvation.

The LORD has been the strength and song for the Israelites, giving them hope and eventually sending Moses to deliver them. Only now, however, does he become their salvation by leading them out of Egypt to the far side of the sea and drowning their oppressors. Israel is completely safe from bondage, delivered from the place of bondage, and from the one who would keep them in bondage. God has stepped into human history, not just to save, but to become salvation. He is always with those who believe, as their strength and song, but he also becomes salvation at this critical moment in Israel's story.

The Song at the Sea is included in the Siddur, toward the end of Pesukei d'Zimrah, the verses of praise that open the daily morning prayers. The Chasidic rabbis (cited by Yitzhak Buxbaum in his book *Jewish Spiritual Practices*) recommend that worshipers employ their imagination especially in reciting the Song. When Rabbi Shmelke of Nikolsburg led the prayers one morning, the congregation "all lifted up the hems of their kaftans to keep them from getting wet, for it actually seemed to them that they had gone down into the Sea which had split before them."

We need to revisit the Splitting of the Sea because it is an incomparable moment in our story as a people, the moment when salvation is not just a promise to be hoped for, nor a remembrance of past victory, but an immediate, present event. God has become salvation to me—*vay'hi li lishu'ah*.

The introduction to the Song provides a further clue to its importance. The Torah says literally, "Then Moses and the children of Israel *will sing* this song to the LORD" (15:1). Rashi explains that just as God intervened in Israel's story at the Splitting of the Sea to become salvation, so he will intervene in Messianic times to raise the dead, becoming salvation again. Then Israel will sing the Song again. Hence, in the Book of Revelation (15:3), as God intervenes at the culmination of history, the redeemed will "sing the song of Moses, the servant of God."

Isaiah develops the picture of this time of salvation, "that day" when the LORD's anger will be turned away and he will comfort Israel. Then he will become salvation again—*vay'hi li lishu'ah* (12:2). In that day, the prophet continues, "With joy you will draw water from the wells of salvation—*mima'ayney ha-yeshu'ah*" (Isa. 12:3).

These verses from Isaiah became the opening words of the Havdalah service. The ending of Shabbat can be a gloomy time, so the Havdalah service sets a tone of hope. Shabbat is a memorial of the departure from Egypt when the LORD became our salvation. At its conclusion, we look forward to the day when he will again become our salvation. Accordingly, the Havdalah opens with Isaiah's prophecy of that day, and ends with the song *Eliyahu HaNavi*, a song of yearning for the prophet Elijah to appear and announce the coming of Messiah.

The third appearance of the verse stirs up similar thoughts. Psalm 118 is a psalm of messianic import, as many early commentators recognized. The psalmist thanks the LORD for his great deliverance, when he goes beyond his normal action in history to "become my salvation"—*vay'hi li lishu'ah* (vs. 14). The psalmist goes on to speak of "the stone which the builders rejected" that "has become the chief cornerstone" (vs. 22). Early followers of Yeshua saw in him the fulfillment of this messianic verse: rejected by the religious authorities of his day he became the foundation of God's "building" from that time on.

Indeed, the very name Yeshua invokes this key verse of the Tanach. The verse proclaims that the God of Israel has personally intervened in Israel's story to bring salvation, and will do so again. Our story as a people begins in divine victory and will culminate in divine victory. When Miriam was carrying the promised Messiah in her womb, an angel told her husband Yosef, "You shall call his name Yeshua, for he will save his people from their sins" (Matt. 1:21). *Yeshua* is the masculine form of the feminine noun "salvation," as in our verse, "He shall become to me salvation." Isaiah adds "You will draw water from the wells of salvation—*yeshu'ah*." The name given to the Messiah reitcrates the promise of a future victory, when God will again become salvation by entering Israel's history to rescue us.

This rescue is launched with the coming of Yeshua of Nazareth, and will be consummated at his return, which completes God's purposes not only for Israel, but for all the nations. At that time, "They sing the song of Moses, the servant of God, and the song of the Lamb, saying:"

Great and wonderful are your works
O Lord God Almighty!
Just and true are your ways,
O king of the nations! . . .
For all nations shall come and worship before you.
(Rev. 15:3–4)

Lessons of the Desert

Parashat Yitro, Exodus 18:1–20:23

*In the third month after the children of Israel wnet
forth from the land of Egypt, on the same day, they
came to the Desert of Sinai. For they departed from
Rephidim, came to the Desert of Sinai, and camped in
the desert. So Israel camped there before the mountain
and Moses went up to God. . . .* (Exod. 19:1–2)

In the story of our deliverance from Egypt, we have come to Mount
Sinai, the holy mountain where Adonai reveals himself to Israel. The
mountain is etched deeply in our imaginations: the thunder and
lightning flashes and a thick cloud hiding its summit as Moses as-
cends to receive the Ten Commandments. With such an image in
mind we may forget that this mountain is in the midst of a desert,
and that Israel, awaiting the revelation of God, is encamped not in
the foothills, but in the descrt opposite the mountain.

The word desert is מדבר—*midbar*—sometimes translated wilderness. It refers to barren places lacking in water and vegetation,
places inhospitable to human presence. Toward the conclusion of
Israel's wanderings, Moses reminds them of "the great and awesome desert, in which were fiery serpents and scorpions and thirsty
land where there was no water" (Deut. 8:15).

The word *midbar* contains the Hebrew root דבר—*dabar*—
meaning word. Desert is the place of the word, the place of revelation. Here the normal props to human pride and comfort fall away.
Our usual distractions are missing. Its very hostility toward the
human suits it as the place to encounter the divine. Indeed, when
Moses first encounters God in the burning bush, it is at this same
place. In that encounter, the place is described as *achar hamidbar*,

on the far side of the desert. The mount of revelation is in the heart of the wilderness.

Moses' early encounter at the burning bush sets in motion the tension of the entire first half of Exodus: out of Egypt and into the desert. Before the encounter ends, God tells Moses that he will send him to lead Israel out of bondage. "And this shall be a sign to you that I have sent you: When you have brought the people out of Egypt, you will serve God on this mountain" (Exod. 3:12). The goal of the Exodus is the mount of revelation in the farthest desert.

The desert is the opposite of Egypt, the place of worldly abundance, human pride, heroic architecture, and the worship of idols. The desert is the terrain that will separate the Israelites from everything Egyptian, so that they can serve a God who is holy: pure, uncorrupted, glorious with a light that transcends the world of human accomplishment. The desert of Sinai is where God first calls Israel to be holy as well: "You shall be to me a special treasure from among all peoples. Indeed, all the earth is mine, but you shall be to me a kingdom of priests and a holy nation" (19:5–6). The journey through the desert to Sinai has prepared Israel for this call.

When Moses first confronted Pharaoh, he had requested leave for a three-day journey into the desert for Israel to sacrifice to their God (5:3). Israel finally leaves Egypt and goes out into the Desert of Shur. "And they went three days in the desert and found no water" (15:22). There, at Marah, they encountered bitter water that they could not drink until God miraculously transformed it. Then they traveled to the Desert of Sin and found no food. Here the miraculous supply of manna began. Finally Israel came to Rephidim and again found no water. Here also the LORD demonstrated his ability to provide. The three-day journey into the desert begins a repeated series of lessons in which Israel learns two essential truths.

First, they find out who they are—vulnerable, dependent, profoundly in need of God. In the desert things become very simple. We encounter thirst and hunger, and our ultimate inability to meet even these basic needs for ourselves.

Egypt, even with its bondage, conspires to deny this truth through its abundant supply of food and water. At moments of weakness throughout their wanderings, the Israelites would continue to long for the provisions of Egypt. "We remember the fish which we ate freely in Egypt, the cucumbers, the melons, the leeks, the onions, and the garlic; but now our whole being is dried up!" (Num. 11:5–6) Egypt is like America and the developed world today. Our abundance deludes us into thinking we are really something in ourselves. The desert reveals our dependency.

Second, in the desert Israel encounters God's faithfulness precisely at their point of dependency. Despite their fears, God did not lead them into the desert to die, but to live in freedom from the false gods of Egypt. It is in our need that we learn to truly rely upon the God of Israel.

Desert is the essential transition. Without this two-fold lesson there will be no encounter with a Holy God. We sometimes imagine a spiritual journey that provides immediate transition from Egypt to Sinai, that separates us from the old ways and brings us into complete revelation without the realities of discipline, trial, and preparation. But we will not *desire* the encounter with a holy God if we still think we are something in ourselves.

The earliest account of the life of Messiah opens in the desert. John is "the voice of one crying in the wilderness" foretold by the prophet Isaiah (Mark 1:3). Like Moses, he calls the Israelites out to the desert to encounter God. They prepare for the encounter by immersing in the Jordan and confessing their sins. Yeshua also goes out to John in the desert and is also immersed, and then goes farther into the desert to be tempted. After the temptation he is ready to go back to the villages and towns of Israel, but he continually returns to the desert to seek God and pray (Mark 1:35, 45; Luke 5:16). As the story goes on, he takes his disciples out to the desert as well. They establish a rhythm of engagement with the needs of the people and withdrawal to the presence of God.

Desert is essential to our formation as a people, and as individuals. We need to embrace desert, silence, and solitude, as sources of spiritual abundance. Other disciplines, such as fasting, abstinence from entertainment, or simply obeying the command to cease from our own works on Shabbat, return us to the desert. There we remember a two-fold lesson: we are vulnerable and dependent, and God meets us in our dependency.

Don't Follow the Crowd

Parashat Mishpatim, Exodus 21:1–24:18

The laws of Torah are remarkable in their refusal to distinguish between what we would term civil and religious matters. At Sinai, the Lord gave Moses a variety of laws that cover many aspects of life—civil, criminal, and ceremonial—as a seamless whole. These laws also tend to ignore our distinction between public and private actions, so that it is sometimes unclear in what context a particular law might apply.

One example is Exodus 23:2: "Do not go after *rabim* (the many or the multitude) for evil . . ." Rashi opens his commentary on this commandment by citing a talmudic discussion that applies it to the practice of jurisprudence. This discussion says that if a panel of judges agrees to acquit a criminal, a simple majority will suffice, but if the panel agrees to convict, it must have a majority of at least two. Another passage in the Talmud argues that the majority of two is required for conviction only in capital cases. In either event, the verse is taken as an instruction to judges: "Do not go after *rabim*, a simple majority, to reach a 'bad' verdict [that is, a conviction]."

Rashi goes on to give the simple meaning of the verse, the *p'shat* or plain sense, as opposed to the *derush*, or detailed interpretation. "If you see wicked people perverting justice, do not say, 'Since they are *rabim* (many), I will follow them.'" By this reading, the verse applies not only to judges in their public office, but to every private individual. It describes a temptation that we all encounter; in modern parlance, peer pressure.

This instruction is especially relevant to us who live in democratic societies. Here, the majority, or *rabim* as in our verse, rules. We are to respect the wishes of the majority and should not lightly contradict them. Yet, the majority may cloud our judgment. In covering last year's impeachment trial of President Clinton, the media often cited polls finding that the majority of Americans approved of Clinton's performance as President, and opposed his removal from office. Whether this opinion was correct or not, it could certainly have great influence in the trial. The Senators were charged to be objective and to judge fairly. To do so would have required that they disregard the many altogether, but is this possible in an open, democratic society?

Furthermore, it is normally commendable to be concerned with the many, or in today's language, to respect the will of the majority. Such respect, however, can make it difficult to discern when the majority might be leading one toward evil. Israel's leaders encountered just this difficulty when the people were encamped opposite Mount Sinai.

Moses had ascended the mountain to receive the stone tablets of the law, and had left Aaron and Hur in charge of the camp (24:14). He spent forty days and nights in the presence of God. When he returned he discovered the people in the midst of an orgy, dancing before a calf made of gold. Who had made such a thing?

Moses confronted Aaron, whom he had appointed to lead the people, only to discover that Aaron had not only permitted the orgy to take place, but had made the calf himself. When the people clamored for a visible god in the absence of their leader Moses, Aaron told them to bring their gold earrings to him. He took the gold, "fashioned it into a molten calf," and then built an altar before it (32:4-5).

Moses demanded of Aaron, "What did this people do to you that you have brought such a great sin upon them?" Aaron replied, "You know that the people are set on evil" (32:21–22). Aaron had followed the majority into evil, instead of leading them away from it.

Aaron is known as a man of peace. "Hillel said, 'Be of the disciples of Aaron, loving peace and pursuing peace, loving your fellow men, and drawing them near to Torah'" (Pirke Avot 1:12). The pursuit of peace will often demand compromise, the ability to go beyond narrow concerns and viewpoints for the sake of preserving community. It will require one to see things from the perspective of another, rather than to dogmatically hold to one's own outlook. But such pursuit of peace is risky, for it can lull a person, whether in a public role as leader, or in a private role, into the sort of compromise that Aaron made, a compromise with evil.

It is easy to imagine that Aaron's motives were good, as many of the rabbinic commentaries insist. Aaron responds to the values of peace and community, which are so deeply embedded in Torah. He wants to keep the people together and soothe their fears in Moses' absence. But, of course, such values are not the ultimate ones. There is something higher—loyalty to the God who called us as a community. Cherishing genuine peace and community may sometimes require one to stand against the people. The leader, or any conscientious individual, must sometimes resist the will of the community to genuinely serve the community. Otherwise he becomes useless: "A righteous man who falters before the wicked is like a murky spring or a polluted well" (Prov. 25:26).

When Moses descended the mountain he saw that the people were unrestrained and exposed to their enemies. The Torah lays responsibility for this disaster at Aaron's feet: "Aaron had not restrained them, to their shame among their enemies" (32:25). The entire account concludes with the words: "So the Lord plagued the people because of what they did with the calf that Aaron made" (32:35).

Aaron exposed the people by heeding their request. Moses confronted the people and judged them harshly, leading the sons of Levi to execute 3000 idolaters in their midst. Only then was he able to effectively intercede with God for mercy upon Israel. Often it is the one who resists the pressure of the many who in the end is able to most benefit them. The one who plays to the crowd risks losing their respect and, worse, his own integrity.

Noble Servitude

Parashat T'rumah, Exodus 25:1–27:19

In the account of our deliverance from Egypt, we have come to the building of the *mishkan,* the portable dwelling for Adonai as he accompanies his people in their wanderings. This tabernacle, with its elaborate construction and furnishings, with the priestly garments and equipment, will dominate the rest of the book of Exodus. Its construction is the culmination of the departure from Egypt. Adonai brought Israel forth from Egypt to serve him, and this is the place of that service.

It is remarkable, then, that this vital and demanding project is to be supplied by voluntary offerings. As he begins his instructions for the mishkan, the Lord tells Moses, "Speak to the children of Israel and let them raise up for me an offering; from every man whose heart moves him, you shall raise up my offering" (Exod. 25:1–2). Every aspect of the project is spelled out in precise detail: "According to all that I show you, the pattern of the mishkan and the pattern of all its vessels, so shall you do" (25:9). Remarkably, the resources for this project are to be gathered by voluntary contributions.

This aspect of the project is even more remarkable in light of the common rabbinic understanding that mandatory obedience is better than voluntary. In this view, it is better to do a deed in obedience to a mitzvah than simply because one wants to. Obedience to a mitzvah involves a degree of understanding and self-discipline that spontaneous action does not. It also, at least ideally, involves the same level of heart motivation that spontaneous action does. Hence, obedience involves more of the whole person in God's service. Why, then, is the gathering of materials for the mishkan left entirely up to voluntary action?

The Torah is teaching here an essential truth about serving the God of Israel.

Before our deliverance, "The Egyptians made the children of Israel serve with crushing hardness. They embittered their lives with hard servitude in mortar and in brick and in every servitude in the field. All their service in which they made them serve was with crushing hardness" (1:13–14). In these two verses the root *avad*, service, labor, servitude, appears five times, and it is clearly compulsory service.

When we retell the Passover story at the seder, we lift our cups and recite, "He brought us out from servitude to freedom . . . Hallelujah!" Passover is called "the season of our freedom." Torah, however, speaks not so much of freedom, as of a change of servitude. We were serving Pharaoh, but the Lord commanded him, "Let my people go that they may serve *me*" (8:1).

In the service of Pharaoh the Israelites are compelled to build with bricks and mortar the store-cities of Pithom and Raamses. In the service of Adonai they willingly build the mishkan, the dwelling place for the Lord who took them out of the house of bondage.

Freedom, our ancient story tells us, is not a matter of total autonomy, or the absence of any authority over one's life. Rather, freedom is servitude to the one true God, the one who is worthy to be served. We enter this freedom by serving willingly, as the Israelites did when each one contributed to the offering voluntarily, as his heart moved him—*yidvenu libo.*

The Hebrew here is instructive. The root of the verb *yidvenu* or "moved" is *nadav*, which also is the root for the noun "noble" or "prince." The connection is clear: a nobleman is one who is free to act as he is moved, not under compulsion. He is not subject to hard labor and oppression, but neither does he live only for himself. Rather, he serves freely, giving his resources and his own self to the cause of a worthy master.

In most of its laws, including those of offerings, the Torah gives rather specific requirements. In this vital offering for a dwelling place for God, however, voluntary giving prevails. Thus, we see that service to the LORD is never oppressive or degrading, as is service to Pharaoh, but instead ennobling.

This view of service counters the modern tendency to glorify human autonomy and to denigrate any submission of self, even submission to the almighty. In an interview in *Moment* magazine (February 1999), Rabbi Sherwin Wine, founder of Humanistic Judaism, stated, "We believe that the power to deal with the problems in our life does not come from some divine or supernatural source, but from within us—me and other people." In such a view, which is undoubtedly far more prevalent than Wine's particular movement, submission to a "divine or supernatural source" would be degrading and pointless. The Torah makes it clear, however, that such submission elevates man.

Yeshua built upon this truth when he stated, "Take my yoke upon you and learn from me . . . for my yoke is easy and my burden is light" (Matt. 11:29–30). Normally a yoke is an instrument of bondage, imposed upon a beast or a man against his will. Yeshua calls us to take the yoke of service voluntarily. Such a yoke he terms "my yoke"; one that unites us to him. We will discover it to be not oppressive, but easy. Freely yielding oneself to God is elevating; serving God instead of self is liberating.

Indeed, the very name of our parasha, T'rumah, points to the same truth. This word refers to the offering for the mishkan. "Speak to the children of Israel and let them raise up for me an offering . . ." Its root is *rum*, "to be high, elevated; to rise up." The offering is raised up to God, but it also raises up the offerer. Service to the God of Israel is elevating.

There is a further lesson in our parasha. Moses' instruction that "every man whose heart moves him" is to give focuses on the individual, as does Yeshua's invitation to take on his yoke. But Scripture does not stop at this individual response to God. Yeshua's invitation to take on his yoke is to "*all* who labor and are heavy laden" (Matt. 11:28). The mishkan is built through the efforts of *all*, the combined response of multitudes of willing hearts.

> And they spoke to Moses saying, "The people bring much more than enough for the service of the work which the Lord commanded to make." And Moses gave command and they announced it throughout the camp, saying: "Let neither man nor woman make any more work for the offering of the sanctuary." So the people were restrained from bringing. For the materials they had were sufficient for all the work to make it, and too much. (36:5–7)

We gain spiritual freedom as we voluntarily serve God. This is the servitude that ennobles, and it is not individual alone, but a shared servitude with all whose hearts move them to give. With such we will build the dwelling that God assigns us.

The Garments of Priesthood

Parashat Tetzaveh, Exodus 27:20–30:10

Now bring near Aaron your brother, and his sons with him, from among the children of Israel, that he may minister to Me as priest, Aaron and Aaron's sons: Nadab, Abihu, Eleazar, and Ithamar. And you shall make holy garments for Aaron your brother, for glory and for splendor. (Exod. 28:1–2)

In his office as *Kohen Gadol*, High Priest, Aaron is clothed in garments of glory and splendor. Glory, of course, belongs to the Lord, but it also shines upon Aaron. All the priests wear four garments—breeches, tunic, turban, and sash—and the High Priest alone wears four additional garments (Yoma 71b). These garments are kingly: a breastplate of gold and precious gems; an ephod, or apron, attached to the shoulders with onyx stones set in gold; a robe dyed with the precious blue of royalty and hemmed with golden bells and pomegranates; and a golden head plate.

The Kohen Gadol is dressed in royal attire. In his own person he fulfills Israel's calling to be *mamlechet kohanim*, a kingdom of priests (Exod. 19:6), or as Shimon later phrases it in Greek, a royal priesthood (1 Pet. 2:9). He is a priest who emanates royalty, who combines in himself the two exalted offices in Israel.

The Talmud tells of an encounter between such a priest and Alexander the Great (Yoma 69a). After Alexander conquered the land of Israel, the Samaritans petitioned him to destroy the Holy Temple. On his way to Jerusalem, he was met by a delegation of Jewish leaders appealing for mercy, led by the High Priest Shimon ha-tzaddik. When Alexander saw Shimon dressed in his priestly garments, he descended from his chariot and bowed down to him.

His Samaritan supporters said, "Such a great king as you are and you bow down to that Jew?" Alexander answered, "His image glistened before me whenever I had a victory"

Alexander recognized royalty and bowed before it. The Talmud is employing irony here: Alexander bows before a mere priest, but the priest represents the one true King, the King of kings. Israel is a royal priesthood, a priestly nation mediating knowledge of the King to all nations . . . in this instance represented by Alexander who has conquered all nations.

In his commentary on the previous parasha, T'rumah, Ramban notes that the tabernacle is designed to be a portable Sinai, preserving the divine encounter at Sinai throughout all of Israel's wanderings. "The secret of the tabernacle is that the glory that abode upon Mount Sinai should abide upon it . . . Thus Israel always had with them in the tabernacle the glory that appeared to them on Mount Sinai." Likewise, a priest clothed like a king preserves Israel's calling at Sinai to be a kingdom of priests, the calling to represent the true King to all the nations.

Shimon writes that this calling will be shared by all who come to Messiah in faith, who are called "out of darkness into his marvelous light" (1 Pet. 2:9). Such a calling, however, has its pitfalls, as any observer of religious life can confirm. The sense of being chosen can fuel vanity and self-righteousness. Priests of whatever faith often savor their own glory and hold themselves above those they are supposed to serve. Recognizing such human frailty, the Torah includes safeguards against spiritual pride within the priestly wardrobe.

Upon the two shoulders of the ephod are two onyx stones set in gold. The names of the sons of Israel are engraved on the two stones, so that Aaron "shall bear their names before the LORD on his two shoulders as a memorial" (28:12). Likewise, the breastplate contains twelve precious stones corresponding to the twelve tribes. "So Aaron shall bear the names of the sons of Israel on the breastplate of judgment over his heart, when he goes into the holy place, as a memorial before the LORD continually" (28:29). The High Priest is a glorious burden-bearer on behalf of the sons of Israel. He must bear their names continually, even in his moment of highest exaltation when he goes into the holy place and appears before the Lord himself.

"Glory" is *kavod* in Hebrew, which also means "heavy" or "weighty." The priestly garments are heavy with glory . . . and with the remembrance of Israel. They teach us that true glory bears tremendous responsibility. If there is a divine calling, it is a calling to serve, to be concerned for our fellow human beings, and to remember them even in our most sublime moments.

Torah provides another safeguard against pride. A priest never lives for himself, and his glory is not his own. The garments lend him glory, but without them, he has none. Hence, the Torah decrees that if he enters God's presence without the garments he is doomed.

> And upon its hem you shall make pomegranates of blue, purple, and scarlet, all around its hem, and bells of gold between them all around: a golden bell and a pomegranate, a golden bell and a pomegranate, upon the hem of the robe all around. And it shall be upon Aaron when he ministers, and its sound will be heard when he goes into the holy place before the LORD and when he comes out, that he may not die. (Exod. 28:33–35, NKJV)

Rashi says that the sound of the bells represents all the priestly garments. It indicates that the priest is wearing them. Therefore, "he will not be subject to the death penalty. But if he enters the holy place lacking one of these garments, he will be subject to death at the hand of Heaven." Ramban disagrees. Other passages make it clear that the High Priest must wear the garments to enter the Holy Place. This passage, he says, is dealing specifically with the bells. Their sound signals the approach of the priest, so that the Master may give him permission to enter in.

> For he who comes into the king's palace suddenly, incurs the penalty of death according to the court ceremonial, just as we find in the case of Ahasuerus [in the Book of Esther]. . . . Similarly, when going out from the Sanctuary his sound is heard in order to leave with permission.

Despite their disagreement on these details, the great commentators agree that the High Priest cannot enter the presence of God on his own merit. If he presumes to do so, he is swiftly cut off. God clothes Aaron with a royal splendor, but he is a servant king and a burdened priest. He bears the sons of Israel upon his shoulders and their names upon his heart with every step he takes. And he has no glory of his own.

The glory in being chosen by God returns to God. Shimon reminds us that "once you were no people but now you are God's people; once you had not received mercy but now you have received mercy" (1 Pet. 2:10). Only through mercy do we qualify as royal priests. The glory we have means "that when the Gentiles speak against you as wrongdoers, they may see your good deeds and glorify God on the day of visitation" (1 Pet. 2:12). We may be tempted to take the glory of our garments for ourselves, but those around us will see only God's mercy and will learn to give the credit to him.

Can a Man See God?

Parashat Ki Tissa, Exodus 30:11–34:35

Can a man see God? After Adonai sealed his covenant with Israel at Mount Sinai, he called Moses and Aaron, Nadav and Avihu, and seventy of the elders of Israel to ascend the mountain. There "they saw the God of Israel" (Exod. 24:10). Indeed, not only did these men see God, but the Torah even describes the appearance of the pavement under God's feet. In the sight of Adonai, the elders ate and drank—probably to celebrate the covenant that had just been sealed. Apparently, Israel's leaders did indeed see God.

Later, however, when Moses asks Adonai to show him his glory, he replies, "You cannot see my face; for no man shall see me and live" (33:20). Ramban comments on this verse:

> This does not mean that a man could see him, but then would immediately die. It means that before a man could grasp the sight of God, his soul would leave him, for even of a vision of the angels it is written, "As a result of the vision anguish has come upon me, and I have retained no strength" (Dan. 10:16b).

If a vision of angels causes such anguish to the prophet, a vision of God himself would kill a man. Ramban says that death does not come later as a consequence of the vision, but is brought on by the vision itself. The sight of God would drive the soul out of a man. The New Covenant Scriptures agree: "No man has seen God at any time" (John 1:18). What then did Moses and the elders—all of whom survived the experience—see on the mountain?

This question grows more complex as we consider a statement Adonai later makes to Miriam and Aaron when they challenge the authority of their brother Moses. Adonai upholds Moses, saying "I speak with him face to face, even plainly, and not in dark sayings; and he sees the face of Adonai" (Num. 12:8).

Moses sees God, but he does not see. He encounters God face to face, but he cannot see God's face. No matter how much of God a man might see, God remains infinitely beyond his seeing. Clearly, Moses senses this paradox. In our parasha, shortly after he ascended Mount Sinai with the seventy elders and "saw the God of Israel," he asks God to show him his glory. The elders may have been satisfied with their vision of God, but Moses—who sees face to face—knows that he has not really seen God. The man of vision knows that his vision is inadequate, and says "Please, show me your glory" (33:18).

God responds, "Behold, there is a place near me. You may stand upon a rock as my glory passes by. I shall place you in a cleft of the rock and shield you with my hand until I have passed by. Then I shall remove my hand and you will see my back, but my face may not be seen" (33:21–23).

The Torah teaches us two lessons in this incident.

First, when God grants Moses his request, he will go beyond visual revelation to verbal revelation. The visual impact will be minimal; instead, Adonai will proclaim his **name**:

> *Adonai, Adonai, El Rachum*—God, compassionate, gracious, slow to anger, abounding in *Chesed V'emet*—grace and truth—showing grace to the thousandth generation, bearing iniquity, transgression and sin, not clearing the guilty, but visiting the iniquity of the fathers upon the children to the third and fourth generation. (34:6–7)

Moses desires to **see** God's glory; instead he **hears** God's name, a description of his character that later became known as the Thirteen Attributes of Mercy. We might expect Adonai to grant Moses' request in an overwhelming display of power, light, and majesty. Instead, to the one who has already seen more than any other prophet, he gives a verbal statement of his faithfulness and compassion.

From this time on, the knowledge of God unfolds verbally, as a millennia-long dialogue between Adonai and his people. Visual revelation is sudden, dramatic, an unrepeated and ultimately indescribable mystical encounter. Verbal revelation, in contrast, is a process, a relationship that develops over time. Furthermore, verbal revelation, far from being indescribable, can be recorded and transmitted to future generations, as it has been in Israel's scriptures.

A second lesson is that, although no human can see him and live, the God of Israel finds a way to make himself more fully known. Scripture is not so much the story of humanity's discovery of God, as it is of God's progressive self-revelation to man. He is not a God who hides himself without cause, or plays cat-and-mouse with man, but a God who seeks to bridge the gap between himself and humankind.

God may not be readily seen in our world; indeed we could not survive a vision of God in his essence. But God does speak to us. After he speaks to Moses of his own nature, Adonai goes on to pronounce covenant requirements upon Israel. God speaks a word not just for the prophets, but for all Israel, and through Israel for all humanity. God is beyond our vision, but he engages us in an ancient dialogue through which we come to understand him more and more fully.

Significantly, God initiates this dialogue not with a description of his awesome power and majesty, but with *chesed v'emet*—grace and truth. The Thirteen Attributes of Mercy are reiterated numerous times throughout Torah and the Prophets, and have become part of the liturgical heritage of Israel. Finally, God intensified the dialogue by sending the Messiah to embody these attributes.

> The Torah was given through Moses; *chesed v'emet*—grace and truth—came through Yeshua the Messiah. No one has ever seen God, but the only and unique Son, who is identical with God, and is at the Father's side—he has made him known. (John 1:17–18, *Jewish New Testament*)

John is not drawing a contrast between Torah and grace, or between Moses and Yeshua. Rather he is describing Yeshua as the living Torah who embodies the very attributes that Adonai declared to Moses. He is the Word of God, God's self-expression, revealed in human form (John 1:1, 14).

Can a human being see God? Never in his essence. But we can hear him. The God who seeks to make himself known has spoken and continues to speak in Torah, and in the living Torah, Yeshua the Messiah.

Creation Restored

Parashat Vayak'hel, Exodus 35:1–38:20

As we approach the conclusion of Exodus, Moses calls the children of Israel together to begin building the tabernacle. First, however, he reminds them that work—מלאכה (*m'lachah*) in Hebrew—may not be done on Shabbat. "Work shall be done for six days, but the seventh day shall be a holy day for you, a Shabbat of rest to Adonai. Whoever does any work on it shall be put to death" (35:2). *M'lachah* appears twenty more times in the final chapters of Exodus to describe the work of building the tabernacle. The Talmud (Shabbat 97b) derives from this connection that the thirty-nine categories of work involved in building the tabernacle are the categories of work forbidden on Shabbat.

The same Hebrew word appears three times at the conclusion of the Creation account (Gen. 2:2–3):

> And on the seventh day God finished His work which He had done, and He rested on the seventh day from all His work which He had done. Then God blessed the seventh day and sanctified it, because in it He rested from all His work that God had created and made.

After the six days of Creation, God instituted the seventh day as the day of rest when he abstained from all his work. In the same way, at the beginning of our parasha, he reiterated the command of Shabbat to the children of Israel to contain and delimit the work of the tabernacle.

The tabernacle, encompassing all the varieties of creative work that are forbidden on Shabbat, is the great act of creation that reflects the original Creation. Sefat Emet, the nineteenth century Chasidic commentator, writes

The whole purpose of making the sanctuary was to affirm Creation. This is the Creation, of which it is said: "And God saw all that He had made, and behold it was very good . . . heaven and earth were completed . . . and God blessed [them] . . ." (Gen. 1:31–2:3). So, too, the sanctuary, which confirms that Creation: "Moses saw . . . and it was good in his sight . . . Moses blessed them." (The Language of Truth, p. 135f.)

In a similar way, the Midrash comments on the command to build the ark, which is the first vessel listed in the construction of the tabernacle.

Just as the Torah preceded everything at the Creation, so also did He give precedence to the Ark over all other vessels in the construction of the tabernacle; and just as light preceded all other works of the Creation, as it says, *And God said: Let there be light* (Gen. 1:3), so also did the work in connection with the Torah, which is called *light*—as it is written, *For the commandment is a lamp, and the teaching is light* (Prov. 6:23)—take precedence over all the other vessels in the construction of the tabernacle. (Exodus Rabbah 34:2)

The message of the tabernacle is that Creation was originally meant to provide a dwelling place of the most high, where God and humankind could meet. But the universe has become disordered; the divine presence is gone, so God provides a model of the Creation where he can meet with the representative humankind, Israel, in the person of the Aaronic priest.

Tabernacle is *mishkan* in Hebrew, from the root שָׁכַן (*shachan*), meaning to dwell. The tabernacle represents the ideal of Creation, which was intended as a dwelling for God where his presence or Shechinah, from the same Hebrew root, might dwell with man.

Thus, in the Garden of Eden before their transgression, the man and the woman were apparently accustomed to meet with God "in the cool of the day" (Gen. 3:8). When the Lord drove Adam and Eve out of the Garden, he placed cherubim at its border to keep them away. In the tabernacle, the Shechinah drew near to man again at the ark of the covenant. Cherubim were placed as guardians of the Shechinah (Exod. 25:22). "And there I will meet with you, and I will speak with you from above the mercy seat, from between the two cherubim which are on the ark of the Testimony . . ."

After Moses gives all the instructions for the tabernacle, the people depart. "Then everyone came whose heart was stirred, and everyone whose spirit was willing, and they brought the LORD's offering for the work of the tabernacle of meeting, for all its service, and for the holy garments" (Exod. 35:21). The people bring such an abundant offering that Moses must issue a proclamation throughout the camp, "Let neither man nor woman do any more work for the offering of the sanctuary." The people had brought materials "sufficient for all the work to be done—indeed too much" (Exod. 36:6–7).

Sefat Emet sees in this incident another parallel between Creation and the tabernacle: "We find in the story of Creation that heaven and earth kept on expanding when they were created, so that God had to stop them and say, 'Enough!' So it was that the children of Israel kept giving until he said to them, 'Enough!'"

Finally, at the conclusion of the building of the tabernacle, the Torah says "And Moses finished the work" (Exod. 40:33). These words reflect the conclusion of the Creation account: "On the seventh day God finished His work."

In time, of course, the tabernacle became the Temple, and the Temple became corrupted and finally destroyed. The prophets look forward to a time when the Temple will be restored in Jerusalem as a source of blessing for all humanity. The prayers of the Siddur cry out repeatedly for this time of restoration, and the whole structure of its liturgy is a reminder of the worship of the Temple. In the New Covenant, the prophet John also looks to the day of restoration (Rev. 21:3–4, NKJV).

And I heard a loud voice from heaven saying, "Behold, the tabernacle of God is with men, and He will dwell with them, and they shall be His people. God Himself will be with them and be their God. And God will wipe away every tear from their eyes; there shall be no more death, nor sorrow, nor crying. There shall be no more pain, for the former things have passed away."

John's vision goes beyond the restoration of the Temple to the original intention of the Temple and the tabernacle before it—to reflect the ideal Creation where God meets with humankind, Creation itself as a holy temple. John sees the holy city descending from heaven, "But I saw no temple in it, for the Lord God Almighty and the Lamb are its temple. The city had no need of the sun or of the moon to shine in it, for the glory of God illuminated it. The Lamb is its light" (Rev. 21:22–23, NKJV).

The Lamb redeems humankind from the transgression inaugurated in the Garden of Eden. Through his intervention, the purpose of Creation is restored, the Shechinah returns, and the Lord God Almighty dwells in the midst of a renewed humanity.

The Cloud of Glory

Parashat P'kudei, Exodus 38:21–40:38

Exodus concludes with the raising of the tabernacle, or *mishkan*, God's dwelling-place in the midst of Israel. When all was completed according to the directions that the Lord gave Moses, "the cloud covered the Tent of Meeting, and the glory of Adonai filled the mishkan. Moses could not enter the Tent of Meeting, for the cloud rested upon it, and the glory of Adonai filled the mishkan" (40:34–35).

The phrase "and the glory of Adonai filled the mishkan" appears twice in these two verses. The sages tell us that the Torah is sparing of words and does not repeat anything without reason. This phrase is repeated because it is the culmination of the entire story of the Exodus from Egypt. Furthermore, the word "cloud" appears five times, once in each of the five final verses of the Book of Exodus. By this, we understand the preeminence of the cloud; it reveals the glory of the God who delivered Israel from Egypt and brought them to himself. The cloud is his presence in the midst of his people.

The cloud of glory has been with Israel throughout most of the Exodus story. It first appeared to the children of Israel in the borderlands of Egypt, as they approached the Sea of Reeds. There the Lord went before them in a pillar of cloud by day and a pillar of fire by night. Undoubtedly there were not two different pillars, but a single pillar that provided both shade by day and light in the darkness of night. This luminous cloud marked the presence of the Lord himself (13:21), or "the angel of God" (14:19). From that time on, Israel followed the cloud in all its wanderings in the wilderness. The cloud that covers the tabernacle is also described, in the final verse of Exodus, as a cloud by day and fire by night.

The glory of the Lord appeared a second time in a cloud after the crossing of the Sea, this time to chastise the Israelites for their grumbling against Moses and Aaron (16:10).

The third manifestation of the cloud of glory is the most dramatic. At Mount Sinai, a cloud descends upon the summit in the sight of all Israel, and God begins to speak to Moses. The sight of the cloud is overwhelming. When the "thick cloud" appears on Sinai, the Lord warns Moses to keep the people at a distance, "lest they break through to gaze at Adonai, and many of them perish" (19:21). The people readily accept this limitation and stand far off while Moses speaks with God. Like the pillar, this is a luminous cloud that also takes on the appearance of fire—and it too is the visible manifestation of the glory of God.

> Then Moses went up into the mountain, and a cloud covered the mountain. Now the glory of Adonai rested on Mount Sinai. . . . The sight of the glory of Adonai was like a consuming fire on the top of the mountain in the eyes of the children of Israel. (24:15–17, NKJV)

Immediately after this description of the glory cloud upon Sinai, the Torah proceeds to give the directions for building the mishkan. In a remarkable insight, Ramban notes the connection between Sinai and the tabernacle:

> The secret of the mishkan is that the glory that abode openly on Mount Sinai would abide on it in a concealed manner. . . . Thus, Israel always had with them in the mishkan the glory that appeared to them on Mount Sinai.

Sinai is the goal of the Exodus, the place of encounter where Israel meets with God and he establishes his covenant with Israel. Such an encounter is a one-time event, but it is also a continuing event that will characterize Israel forever. Sinai will remain with Israel in the form of the mishkan—a portable Sinai. The tabernacle will not only enshrine the tablets of the covenant that Moses brought down from the mountain, but it will reflect the very glory of God that Israel first beheld there.

Ramban says that the glory abides in the mishkan "in a concealed manner." The glory that was revealed openly upon Mount

Sinai now dwelt within the Holy of Holies, hidden from the Israelites, and accessible only to the High Priest on Yom Kippur. At the inauguration of the tabernacle, however, the glory was not concealed, but visible as a cloud that covered the tabernacle so that no one could enter in. Likewise at the inauguration of the Temple of Solomon, the cloud of glory filled the Temple, so that no one could enter (2 Kings 8:10–11).

As at Mount Sinai, the cloud that displays God's glory keeps man at a distance.

The cloud reappears in the days of Messiah. Just as Moses took his disciple Joshua with him when he ascended Sinai, so Yeshua led his closest disciples up to "a high mountain" to pray (Matt. 17:1). When Moses came down from Sinai, the skin of his face shone from the encounter with God's glory, and the people were afraid to come near him (Exod. 34:29ff.). On this other mountain, Yeshua's appearance was transformed "and his face shone like the sun" (Matt. 17:2). Then Moses, with Elijah the prophet, appeared and spoke with him. Yeshua's disciple Shimon suggested that they build, not just a tabernacle, but three tabernacles to mark the event. Shimon made this suggestion "because he did not know what to say, for they were greatly afraid" (Mark 9:6). Perhaps the impulsive disciple had in mind the portable Sinai of the tabernacle in the wilderness. As at Sinai, the encounter with God's glory is awe inspiring, and men want to keep their distance.

As Shimon's words trailed off, "a bright cloud," the luminous cloud of glory, overshadowed them and a voice came out of the cloud—another reminder of Sinai. This time, however, the words were different. God had already spoken the Ten Words that were written on the tablets. He had already given the precepts and instructions of Torah. Now he added only this: "This is my beloved son, in whom I am well pleased. Hear him!" (Matt. 17:5)

The glory cloud was no longer concealed, but rested upon the Messiah. The disciples fell on their faces in awe of the cloud that displays God's glory, but keeps man at a distance. But then Yeshua drew near, touched them, and said "Arise, and do not be afraid" (Matt. 17:7). When they looked up, he alone was there.

וַיִּקְרָא
The Book of Leviticus

As with all the books of Torah, the Hebrew name for Leviticus provides a framework for understanding the entire book. Vayikra means "and he called." Throughout Leviticus, God calls Moses, and all Israel—all those he has redeemed from the bondage of Egypt—to himself as the holy and exalted One.

To allow Israel to draw near despite their sins, God provides a system of priesthood and sacrifice, which is presented in the first and larger half of the book. This presentation culminates in the laws of the Day of Atonement in Chapter 16, the one day of the year when the representative Israelite, the High Priest, may come into the very presence of the Lord.

The second, and shorter, half of Leviticus begins in Chapter 18. This section presents the laws of holiness and justice that will govern the people who have been called to God. The book concludes with a promise of blessing for obedience and a warning of cursing for disobedience, followed by an appendix, Chapter 27, concerning assessments and tithes.

Leviticus continues the themes of Genesis and Exodus: blessing, covenant, divine justice, and the service of worship. And it contributes an additional theme: holiness. This concept has been present in the earlier books, of course, but it is developed fully in Leviticus. Indeed, it could be understood as the theme of the entire book.

Holiness refers first to God's nature as pure, glorious, and utterly other than the created order. When God describes himself as holy, he means that he has a splendor and purity that are not dependent upon, or comparable to, any of the qualities of earth. He cannot be corrupted or compromised by anything. Second, holiness refers to the character of God's chosen people. He makes them holy by choosing them from among all the nations of the earth, and giving them a distinct way of life and service. He also requires them to maintain their purity and to live in obedience to his instruction.

All of this is summed up in one verse, "You shall be holy, for I the Lord your God am holy" (19:2). "I the Lord your God am holy" provides the basis for the sacrificial system of the first half of Leviticus. A holy God requires holy worship and a holy priesthood. "You shall be holy" is the theme of the second half, with its detailed laws that define a way of life for the chosen people.

Leviticus is the shortest of the five books of Moses, comprising only ten parashiyot, and covering just over a year when the Israelites were encamped before Mount Sinai. Indeed, it is the only book of Torah that is set entirely at Mount Sinai, and it is the middle of Torah, with two books preceding it, and two following. These factors, along with the emphasis on holiness, place Leviticus at the very heart of Torah.

The Call Across the Divide

Parashat Vayikra, Leviticus 1:1-5:26

Vayikra, the Book of Leviticus, begins with the words *vayikra el Moshe*, "And he called to Moses . . ." Normally, when God speaks to Moses, the Torah employs the Hebrew verb *amar* or *davar*. *Vayyomer Adonai*, "and the Lord spoke," is a common formula throughout the Torah. *Vayikra*, on the other hand, is used to describe God's speaking to Moses at only three points in the story.

The first vayikra comes at the Burning Bush. Moses is in the wilderness tending the flock of his father-in-law Yitro when he sees a bush burning without being consumed by the fire. He turns aside from the flock to observe it more closely. "Adonai saw that he turned aside to see and God called out to him—*vayikra elav Elohim* —from the midst of the bush and said 'Moses! Moses!' and he replied '*Hineni*—here I am!'" (Exod. 3:4)

The second vayikra comes twice at Mount Sinai. As soon as Israel arrives at the mountain, "Moses went up to God and Adonai called to him—*vayikra elav*—from the mountain" (Exod. 19:3). And again, after Adonai speaks the Ten Words and the first series of instructions to Moses and the people agree to obey them, Moses goes back up the mountain to receive the stone tablets. "Moses ascended the mountain and the cloud covered the mountain. The glory of Adonai rested upon Mount Sinai, and the cloud covered it for six days. And he called to Moses—*vayikra el-Moshe*—on the seventh day from the midst of the cloud" (Exod. 24:15–15). There are two callings at Mount Sinai, but the circumstances around them are nearly the same.

The third vayikra comes here at the beginning of our parasha. To understand it properly, we need to see Vayikra, Leviticus, as a continuation of the story of Exodus. Exodus concludes with the tabernacle or Tent of Meeting in place, erected according to the instructions that God gave to Moses. The glory-cloud of God's presence fills the Tent of Meeting so that Moses cannot go in. In this context, we read the opening words of Vayikra: "And he called to Moses, and Adonai spoke to him from the Tent of Meeting. . ."

The Midrash (Vayikra Rabbah I.7) likewise connects the opening of Leviticus with the conclusion of Exodus.

> What is written prior to this subject? The section of the Tabernacle, [every paragraph concluding,] *Even as the Lord commanded Moses.* This may be compared to [the case of] a king, who commanded his servant, saying to him, 'Build me a palace.' On everything he built he wrote the name of the king; he built the walls, and wrote on them the name of the king; he built pillars, and wrote on them the name of the king; he roofed it with beams, and wrote on them the name of the king. After some time the king entered the palace, and on everything he saw he found his name written. Said he: 'All this honour has my servant done me, and I am within, whilst he is without! Call him, that he may come right in.' So, too, when the Holy One, blessed be He, said to Moses: 'Make me a Tabernacle,' he [i.e. Moses] wrote on everything he made *'Even as the Lord commanded Moses'.* Said the Holy One, blessed be he: "Moses has done Me all this honour, and I am within whilst he is without! Call him, that he may enter the innermost [part of the Tabernacle].' Therefore it is said, AND THE LORD CALLED UNTO MOSES.

Whether because of Moses' faithful service, or because of his own grace, God desires to bring Moses near. He calls across the distance that separates them, the distance of his otherness and awe. The glory-cloud keeps Moses at a distance; the voice of Adonai calls him near.

This same dynamic is at work in the other two calls of Adonai. At the Burning Bush, God appears to Moses as transcendent and awe-inspiring. The fire of God keeps him at a distance, but the voice of God calls to him across the distance. This is holy ground, but God calls Moses into dialogue with the Almighty. Likewise at

Sinai; the appearance is awesome; the glory-cloud covers the mountain and no one can approach. But the voice of God calls Moses to come near and gives him the instructions that will guide Israel from then on.

God calls to Moses across the distance of his holiness. He cannot diminish the impact of his holiness, but he still seeks to bring humanity near. Here is a remedy to our tendency to reduce the divine to our own terms, to produce a user-friendly god. The God of Israel will always transcend our understanding, but he has called to us across that divide. Spiritual development means learning to recognize God's transcendence, as well as learning to hear his call across the divide.

This divine intention is evident in the first words that Adonai speaks to Moses after he calls him. "Speak to the children of Israel and say to them, 'When a man among you brings an offering to Adonai, you shall bring your offering of the livestock, of the herd and of the flock'" (Lev. 1:2). The word for "offering" is *korban*, from the root *karav*, meaning to come or be near. Through the offering, the children of Israel can come near to God, even though his holiness would keep them at a distance. Indeed, the root *karav* appears twice in this one verse, for it also forms the verb translated as "bring." Literally then our verse says, "When a man among you brings near a near-offering . . ."

God calls to Moses across the distance of his holiness and gives him instructions on how one can draw near to the holy. The offering itself bridges the distance between man and God, for it is korban, that which comes near, and a man must come near to present it.

Worship is the goal of the Exodus from Egypt. Why then does the Torah seem to make worship so difficult in the Book of Leviticus? Surely it is our understanding that is at fault; the rules of offering do not make worship more difficult; rather they make it possible. There is a vast gulf between man and God. God calls to man (or his representative Moses) across that gulf to provide a way for man to worship him.

How different is this understanding of the sacrificial system of Leviticus from the typical modern view. We tend to see the elaborate requirements and regulations of sacrifice as creating a distance between man and God. In our enlightened times, we like to em-

phasize the approachability of the divine. After all, God is everywhere, and we can always draw near to him. Hence, we see the altar
and priesthood as impediments, relics of a bygone era.

In the context of Torah, however, altar and priesthood are precisely the opposite. God is everywhere, but his holiness keeps us at
a distance. The Levitical system is given, not to impose or maintain
the distance, but to bring us near. This perspective inevitably alters
our view of our current spiritual circumstance. If altar and priesthood served not to create a barrier between man and God, but to
bridge the barrier, what is our situation now that they have passed
away? What, or who, will bring us near to the holy God?

The Law of Continuity

Parashat Tzav, Leviticus 6:1–8:36

In a recent article in *Moment* (April, 2000), Debra B. Darvick writes, "What we see everywhere is Jews searching for a way to live Jewishly; Jews who had it and lost it, Jews who never had it and want it, converts who have chosen it and are determined to make good their commitment." The article suggests that "to live Jewishly" means finding ways to incorporate Jewish tradition in the midst of our very modern lives. This week's parasha underscores this point.

Moses instructs the priests to begin their day of service in the tabernacle by removing from the altar the ashes of the previous day's offering. This offering was the *olah*, the offering that was completely burned upon the altar and described as "a fire-offering of pleasing aroma to Adonai" (Lev. 1:9). The priest would remove its ashes, or at least a representative portion of them, and place them on the ground next to the altar. He then would change out of his priestly garments into other garments and take the ashes outside the camp to a ritually pure place. Some commentators see these two actions as completely separate; the daily removal of ashes from the altar was a different ritual from the removal of ashes outside the camp. Nevertheless, the significance remains: the priests could not present the daily offering until they had given the remains of the previous day their proper respect.

The ashes are only remains of a past offering, but they are not mere refuse. They retain a trace of the holiness the offering possessed as it was presented upon the altar. The command to respect the ashes reminds us that the past must be honored. Moreover, it teaches that the new day's work cannot begin **until** the past is honored. The ashes have no place in the new day's offering, but they must be properly disposed of before the new offering is presented. This law ensures continuity in the cycle of offerings.

Today continuity of the Jewish community is a profound concern. Various polls and surveys indicate that the Jewish population in the Diaspora, and especially America, is shrinking under the pressures of secularism and assimilation. The underlying question is whether it is worthwhile to remain part of the Jewish people, or as author Darvick puts it, to live Jewishly. For those who are more deeply informed by Scripture than by modern thinking the answer is clear: Jewish continuity is not just a social concern, but reflects the divine purpose for his people. Remaining part of the Jewish people means honoring the Jewish past, refusing to consign it to the dust heap, but respecting it by seeking to learn and remember its lessons. Only then are we ready for the work of a new day.

How do we show respect to the past? One way is through the proper handling of tradition. Tradition honors the past by giving it a voice in the present. We must live in the present, but proper traditions ensure that the past does not become irrelevant or merely antiquarian.

In our time of intense and rapid change, it takes effort to maintain Jewish tradition, but the effort is worthwhile. It frees us from our isolation and grants us membership in a community that spans time as well as distance. Tradition invites the wisdom of the past into our lives. Thus, for example, it provides specific ways to celebrate Shabbat or Passover, rounding out the picture given in Scripture with rituals, songs, menus, and customs. Tradition also grants a new perspective on the issues of the day, so that our thinking is not one-dimensional and subject to the latest trends, but informed by the collective experience of our people.

Traditions are flexible and will always need adaptation to new circumstances. The question is **how** we adapt tradition. Do we handle it with reverence, or with the arrogant carelessness that reinvents tradition to accommodate the tastes of the hour? When we treat the past with respect, we can address the present with flexibility and energy. Proper handling of the past promotes continuity, even as it permits change and adaptation.

This week's parasha provides another key to continuity. While the priest was removing the ashes, a fire remained upon the altar. The command to keep the fire burning was so important that the

Torah gives it three times, in 6:2, 6:5, and finally 6:6. "A permanent fire shall be kept burning upon the altar; it shall not go out!" The ashes are removed day by day, but the fire is permanent.

Continuity requires that something remains the same in the midst of all the changes that assail us. The Torah calls the flame on the altar *aish tamid*, the eternal flame, as it calls the light of the menorah in the tabernacle *ner tamid*, the eternal light (Exod. 27:20). Rashi comments that the fire of the aish tamid provides the flame to light the ner tamid. This unchanging light symbolizes the Torah, God's eternal word to Israel. We use the same name for the light over the ark of the Torah in our synagogues—ner tamid, the eternal light, representing the unchanging flame of Torah.

The mystery of Torah is that, though it is ancient, it belongs not to the past but to the present. Every year as we go through the cycle of Torah readings we discover something new, something uniquely fitted to the needs of the day. The conflict between Isaac and Ishmael provides insight into the Jewish-Arab conflict in the land of Israel. Exodus provides the vocabulary for the Jewish emigration from the former Soviet Union during the past two or three decades. The detailed rulings of Parashat Mishpatim or K'doshim continue to guide us in our daily lives.

The flame, in contrast to the ashes, exists in the present. It may be old, but it is ageless. Thus, Scripture always has an immediate authority. Jewish tradition generally invokes Scripture to explain or validate its origins, but Scripture requires no outside point of validation, and it continues to inform Jewish thinking in all ages, even our own.

These two requirements—honoring the ashes of past offerings and sustaining an ever-present flame—safeguarded the continuity of worship in the tabernacle, and centuries later, in the temple. Honoring the past and maintaining a vital connection with the revealed Scriptures also provides for Jewish continuity in our day.

Strange Fire

Parashat Sh'mini, Leviticus 9:1–11:47

What is the sin of Nadav and Avihu? "They brought before Adonai a strange fire that he had not commanded them. And a fire came forth from before Adonai and consumed them, and they died before Adonai" (Lev. 10:1–2). The brothers' penalty is so severe and the charge against them so briefly stated that commentators have discussed this question for centuries. They brought strange fire before Adonai; but what made it strange?

One theory is that Nadav and Avihu were drunk. Immediately following the account of their sin and punishment, Moses instructs Aaron and his surviving sons to abstain from wine and strong drink when they come into the Tent of Meeting (10:9).

> This may be compared to the case of a king who had a faithful attendant. When he found him standing at tavern entrances, he severed his head [without disclosing the reason], and appointed another attendant in his place. We would not know why he put the first to death, but for his enjoining the second thus: "You must not enter the doorway of taverns"; whence we know that for such a reason he had put the first to death. Thus . . . we would not know why Nadav and Avihu died, but for his commanding Aaron, "Drink no wine nor strong drink." (Leviticus Rabbah 12:1)

Ramban objects to this interpretation. He points out that it would have been unjust of God to punish Nadav and Avihu so severely for violating a commandment that he had not yet given. Rather, he believes that we must look for the meaning of their transgression in the strange fire itself, since it is for this that Torah condemns them. Ramban agrees that the brothers had been drinking. Because of their intoxication, they brought strange fire; this, not the intoxication itself, was the problem. Moses forbade strong drink to prevent the kind of sin into which Nadav and Avihu fell.

Ramban sees the clue to the meaning of the sin in the precise Hebrew wording. "Each took his censer and put fire in it and laid incense on it [literally, 'on her']." To what does the "her" refer? Ramban says that it refers to divine justice, perhaps because this is a feminine noun in Hebrew, *tzedakah*. The brothers brought fire "and directed their thoughts only to this [the attribute of justice], and thus it was not *a fire-offering of a sweet savor* (Lev. 1:9). This is the sense of the expression, *and they laid 'aleha' (upon her) incense*." In other words, Nadav and Avihu presented their offering not to Adonai in his unity and wholeness, but to their own concept of Adonai. This may seem a mere technicality, for how do we ever know whether we are presenting an offering to God as he is, or to our own limited concept of God? Further, the death penalty seems too harsh for those who only erred in their theology. But Nadav and Avihu were guilty of misrepresenting the One whom they as priests were charged to represent before the people, and this is a severe transgression indeed.

Today we are more liable to emphasize God's love and mercy at the expense of his justice—a more compassionate emphasis, but one that still misses the wholeness and unity of Adonai. The word translated as "strange" is *zarah*, which can refer also to an alien or outsider, or to the foreign gods of the heathen. It is the word used in Proverbs to describe the adulteress or the prostitute. The fire is "strange" because it is something holy that is prostituted to a particular human agenda. It appears in the holy place, but fulfills an unholy purpose. It is somehow foreign to the atmosphere of worship of the true God.

As the fire is instrumental in the sin of Nadav and Avihu, so the punishment also involves fire: "A fire came forth from before Adonai and consumed them." This same wording appears two verses earlier. There, after Aaron and his sons were consecrated as priests, Moses and Aaron went out from the Tent of Meeting and blessed the people. Then "a fire came forth from before Adonai and consumed the offering" (9:24).

Fire is a sign of God's presence and power. God had told the priests that he, or his glory, would appear to them that day (9:4, 6).

Then fire came forth from him and "all the people saw it" (9:24).

Strange fire may be something that gives the impression of divine presence, but is of strictly human origin. It is fire that "he had not commanded them" (10:1). The priests minister in a divine-human cooperation; they have a vital part to play in Israel's worship, but they must represent God accurately. They must not replace the ineffable deity with their own limited definitions. Those who are closest to the divine service must be most aware of this boundary between the divine and the human.

Moses tells Aaron, "Adonai spoke of this, saying, 'I will be sanctified through those who are close to me, and I will be honored before all the people'" (10:3). Ramban explains that this saying does not actually appear in so many words in the Torah. Instead,

> Moses said here: "This incident is that which God decreed, 'saying to His heart': *Through them that are nigh unto Me I will be sanctified* so that they should not break forth in My sanctuary; *and before all the people I will be glorified,* so that they treat my dwelling-place with respect."

"This incident," the incursion of the divine fire, is God's statement that those who handle divine matters must treat them with the utmost respect. The fire of God is to have preeminence, not the "strange fire" of religious presumption. This is a sobering lesson in a day when many claim so lightly to speak for God. Thus Ya'akov writes in his letter, "My brothers, let not many of you become teachers, knowing that we shall receive a stricter judgment" (James 3:10).

Moses himself learns the same lesson at the waters of Meribah (Num. 20:9–13). The Israelites complain because there is no water. The Lord tells Moses to speak to the rock, and it will bring forth water. Instead, Moses castigates the people for their constant complaining and strikes the rock. Water comes forth, but the Lord says to Moses, "Because you did not trust me enough to sanctify me in the eyes of the sons of Israel, therefore you shall not lead this congregation into the land that I have given them." As Moses had explained to Aaron after the death of his sons, the Lord "will be sanctified through those who are close to him, and he will be honored before all the people."

People who claim a deep commitment to God sometimes cause offense, not because of their great piety, but because they handle the things of God so glibly. Religious leaders are sometimes rejected, not because a rebellious multitude resists their prophetic words, but because they misrepresent God. Those who are chosen to represent God must take great care in how they speak of divine matters. Those who dwell nearest the fire must give it the greatest respect.

Cleansing the Leper

Parashat Tazria, Leviticus 12:1–13:59

And the leper in whom the plague is, his clothes shall be rent, and the hair of his head shall go loose, and he shall cover his upper lip, and shall cry: "Unclean, unclean." All the days wherein the plague is in him, he shall be unclean. He is unclean; he shall dwell alone; outside the camp shall his dwelling be. (Lev. 13:45–46)

The Hebrew word we translate as "leprosy"—*tzara'at*—apparently comprised a number of different skin diseases. All such diseases, however diverse, threatened the holiness of the camp of Israel. Therefore, the priests were responsible to examine the one who showed any sign of tzara'at and declare him either afflicted or well. "It is a decree of Scripture," writes Rashi, "that there is neither impurity of afflictions of tzara'at nor their purification except by the word of a priest."

The fate of one whom the priest pronounced impure was grave. He was banned from the camp and assigned the clothing of a mourner. He was required to announce his own uncleanness wherever he went, crying "Tamei, Tamei!" so that no one would be involuntarily polluted. Even if a leper thought that he had become free of his disease, he was not to rejoin the people until a priest came to him "outside the camp" (14:3) to examine him and declare him clean.

The ancient commentators tended to see tzara'at as a direct punishment for sin. The leper took on the appearance of a mourner because he was to mourn for his sins that had brought him to this state. He remained outside the camp morally as well as physically, suffering not only from disease, but also disgrace.

Once during the ministry of Messiah, a leper violated these rules. Yeshua was preaching and healing the sick in a Galilean village when a leper came to him, knelt before him and implored, "If you want to, you can make me clean." Yeshua was moved with compassion. He reached out his hand, touched the man in apparent disregard of his uncleanness, and said, "I do want to: be cleansed." And immediately the leprosy left him and he was cleansed (Mark 1:40–41).

In light of the prevailing view of leprosy, Yeshua's contemporaries would be shocked that he let this leper draw near, and even more that he reached his hand out to touch him. Then Yeshua did something his contemporaries might understand, but that we find remarkable. He said to the leper, "Do not tell anyone about this, but go show yourself to the priest and present the offering for your cleansing that Moses required, as a testimony to them" (Mark 1:44).

If Messiah himself cleanses the leper, what need is there for a priest? Torah teaches that when one is cleansed of leprosy, he is to stand outside the camp until the priest comes to examine him and declare him clean. Like the Messiah, such a priest was to receive the leper who presented himself to him. The priest, however, could not cleanse him, and would certainly not touch him. His role was strictly to examine and verify that the leper was cleansed, and then to see that he offered a proper sacrifice to confirm his cleansing. But he has no authority to cleanse; only Messiah possesses that.

Here we see two different authorities. The Messiah has kingly authority to change things, to heal, to drive out evil spirits, to forgive sin. The priest has authority to teach, to judge, to evaluate. These two roles are not necessarily in conflict—Yeshua sends the leper to the priest—but they are quite distinct.

Priestly authority is needed to teach and apply Scripture, to make decisions, to maintain values and tradition. Without priestly authority, we would have little sense of community, and would soon fall into religious anarchy.

Priestly authority can be wielded by a true and a false priesthood. A false priest serves the political or religious establishment. He will call the clean unclean and the unclean clean if it suits the powers of the day. The true priest discerns the underlying spiritual reality; he declares the leper pure because he is indeed pure. Such priesthood might well work in harmony with the kingly authority of the Messiah. So, Yeshua tells the leper to report to the priest "as a testimony to them," to show that he is now clean and can return to the community.

"As a testimony to them," however, can mean something more—that the priestly authority is encountering kingly authority. The cleansing of the leper demonstrates that one is here who has messianic powers. Such cleansing occurred only twice in the Tanach, and the rabbis said it was as hard to cleanse a leper as to raise the dead. The Midrash says, "In this world the priest examines for leprosy, but in the World to Come—says the Holy One, blessed be he—'I will render you clean.' Thus it is written, *And I will sprinkle clean water upon you, and ye shall be clean* (Ezek. 36:25)" (Leviticus Rabbah 15.9).

Priests have great authority, but only kingdom authority can transform lives. This transformation is a testimony that the powers of the age to come have drawn near. And it may become a testimony **against** the priests if they certify this cleansing and then fail to acknowledge Yeshua as Messiah.

As followers of Messiah, we bear kingdom authority, but we're not always willing to touch the lepers. We join the debate over issues such as homosexuality, abortion, or drug abuse to defend the perspective of Scripture. The secular community has largely played the role of a false priest and said to various classes of sinners, "You are not unclean, you are not a leper." We rightly object to such rulings, but we are called to go beyond this debate. We are to touch the leper, not to keep him at a distance with our pronouncements. We sometimes seem more interested in the priestly role of declaring the leper unclean than in our kingdom authority to touch him and see him transformed. If Messiah touched us, we can touch others.

The Sickness of Slander

Parashat M'tzora, Leviticus 14:1–15:33

The condition termed in the Torah *tzara'at* is usually translated as "leprosy," but the Torah's description of it is puzzling if we see it as strictly a medical condition. The various symptoms described do not correspond to the symptoms of leprosy as we know it, or to any other condition known to modern medicine. Furthermore, this version of leprosy is a disease that afflicts not only human beings, but also houses and clothing!

Because tzara'at is apparently not a simple medical issue, the rabbis saw it as a spiritual condition, a punishment for sin, the visible outworking of an inner disorder. Ramban summarizes this perspective in his commentary on Leviticus 13:47, noting that the leprosy described in Torah "is not in the natural order of things, nor does it ever happen in the world outside Israel."

> But when Israel is wholly devoted to God, then His spirit is upon them always, to maintain their bodies, clothes, and houses in a good appearance. Thus as soon as one of them commits a sin or transgression, a deformity appears in his flesh, or on his garment, or in his house, revealing that God has turned aside from him.

The sages of the Talmud went further. They not only claimed that tzara'at is the result of sin, but specified the variety of sin that leads to it. Leper in Hebrew is *m'tzora*, which can be read as a contraction of *motzi ra*, one who brings forth or spreads evil [speech], a slanderer (Arachin 15b).

> Our rabbis have said, "Why is the leper different from others who are impure, so that he must stay in isolation? Since he caused separation through malicious talk—between a man and his wife and between a man and his friend—he too shall be set apart." (Arachin 16b)

Leprosy, then, is the result of *lashon hara*, evil speech, which includes gossip, slander, and divisive talk.

This understanding of leprosy may stem from an incident recorded in the Book of Numbers. Aaron and Miriam challenge the leadership of Moses, saying, "Has the LORD indeed spoken only through Moses? Has He not spoken through us also?" (12:2) The Lord rises to Moses' defense, describing his unique spiritual status and concluding, "Why then were you not afraid to speak against My servant Moses?" (12:10) Immediately Miriam is stricken with leprosy, because she was the one who had instigated the complaints against Moses. She must be "set apart" as the passage above describes, because she has caused separation between Aaron and herself on one hand and Moses on the other. Even after the Lord responds to Moses' prayer for her healing, she must remain outside the camp seven days.

So, leprosy in the Torah is no ordinary disease, but is the visible punishment for a spiritual sickness. Hence, when the leper is healed, he must follow a complex ritual supervised by the priest before he can be declared clean and restored to his people.

The first element of the ritual involves "two live, clean birds, cedar wood, scarlet, and hyssop."

> And the priest shall command that one of the birds be killed in an earthen vessel over running water. As for the living bird, he shall take it, and the cedar wood, and the scarlet, and the hyssop, and shall dip them and the living bird in the blood of the bird that was killed over the running water. And he shall sprinkle upon him that is to be cleansed from the leprosy seven times, and shall pronounce him clean, and shall let the living bird go into the open field. (Lev. 14:4–7, NKJV)

The disease of tzara'at came about through malicious talk, which the Talmud compares to the mindless chattering of birds. Therefore purification ritual from tzara'at requires birds to be effective (Arachin 16b).

But why is one bird killed and the other set free? The Sefat Emet offers a profound insight in his commentary on this parasha.

> The birds are there to atone for two sins. The one that is slaughtered is there so that one will cut himself off from idle chatter, and much more from evil talk itself. The bird that is set free is to prepare the mouth and tongue to speak words of Torah. . . . This bird points to pure speech, which is the very essence of the human being. The verse ". . . man became a living soul" (Gen. 2:7) is translated: "a speaking spirit. . . ."

It is said that gossip has three victims: the one being gossiped about, the one who gossips, and the one who listens. Gossip, then, is a sin of omission as well as a sin of commission. The one who listens to gossip sins by not speaking out against it. In our practical experience we find it easier to refrain from gossip than to speak up and take a stand against gossip when we hear it. We may not say anything ourselves, but until we speak out against *lashon hara*, we are accessories to it.

This is the lesson of the live bird. It reminds us of our uniquely human ability to reflect divine truth through our words. We are not only to avoid speaking harmful words, but to bring pure into any conversation and thereby transform it. When we fail to do so, even if we have spoken no falsehood ourselves, we sin. The consequence of such sin is no longer visible among us as tzara'at, but the more subtle consequences—distrust, disrespect, alienation, fear – are evident all around us.

The live bird reminds us of the God-given power of speech, and our obligation to use it well. As Solomon wrote (Proverbs 18:21), "Death and life are in the power of the tongue, and those who love it will eat its fruit."

Garments of Glory

Parashat Acharei Mot, Leviticus 16:1–18:30

Thus Aaron shall come into the Holy Place: with a young bull as a sin offering, and a ram as a burnt offering. He shall put the holy linen tunic and the linen breeches on his body; he shall gird himself with a linen sash, and the linen turban he shall wear. These are holy garments. Therefore he shall wash his body in water, and put them on. (Lev. 16:3–4)

The High Priest possessed two sets of holy garments. The set he normally employed was the *bigdey zahav* or vestments of gold (Mishnah, Yoma 3.4), consisting of eight items: breeches, tunic, turban, and sash in common with the other priests, and four additional garments worn only by the High Priest. These garments all contained gold: breastplate, ephod, robe hemmed with golden bells and pomegranates, and a golden head plate. Only on Yom Kippur would the High Priest wear the second set of garments, *bigdey lavan* or vestments of white (Yoma 3.6). These were the four garments shared with the ordinary priests, all of white linen.

When the High Priest enters the Holy of Holies on Yom Kippur and appears before the ark of the covenant, he wears the vestments of white. When he concludes this part of the service and comes again before the congregation of Israel, he wears the vestments of gold.

The sages put forth a number of reasons why the High Priest puts aside the gold garments during Yom Kippur. The ordinances for the holy day were given shortly after the sin of the golden calf, and Rashi explains that this sin remains as a prosecutor or accuser against Israel, demanding that Israel be punished. During the crucial moments of the service, when the High Priest is seeking atonement and forgiveness for Israel, it would be inappropriate for him to wear gold that would serve as a reminder of the calf. As the Talmud states, "A prosecutor cannot become an defender" (Rosh Hashanah 26a).

According to most of the commentators, the vestments of white are identical to the vestments of the ordinary priests. This signifies that the High Priest comes before the Lord within the Holy Holies humbly and simply. He does not come in the outward splendor of gold and rich colors, but in pure white. Furthermore, white is the color of forgiveness, and forgiveness is what the High Priest is seeking for himself and all Israel as he comes before the Ark.

The vestments of white are so pure that they must be worn only once. When the High Priest comes out of the Holy of Holies for the last time on Yom Kippur, the Torah says "he shall take off the linen garments that he had worn when he entered the holy place and he shall leave them there" (16:23). Rashi explains that he puts the garments aside and they are never worn again. To further express the unique holiness of the vestments of white, the High Priest again washes himself in water when he removes them, before putting back on the vestments of gold.

Rashi hints at another reason for putting aside the vestments of gold. He distinguishes between the High Priest's "inside service" within the Holy of Holies and in other rituals unique to Yom Kippur, and his usual "outside service." For the inside service, the High Priest wears only white; for the outside service, in the presence of the rest of the priests, the Levites, and all Israel, he wears gold. Within the Holy of Holies, the High Priest appears as a mere mortal; when he returns outside, he reflects the glory of the Holy of Holies in the presence of the people.

In his vestments of gold, the High Priest wears the same materials as the tabernacle itself. Immediately following the instructions for making the tabernacle, Moses turns to the instructions for the garments of the High Priest. These are made of the same "woven linen and blue, purple, and scarlet thread" as the inner covering of the tabernacle, the veil before the Ark, and the screen before the door (Exod. 26:1, 31, 36). In addition, the priestly garments contain threads of gold, which are a reminder of the various golden utensils and fittings of the holy sanctuary.

The breastplate evokes the Holy of Holies: its square shape recalls the multiple squares of the Holy of Holies, which is a cube, and it is made of gold like the ark. Within it are the *urim* and *tummim*, through which the Lord would give instructions to the priests, just as he would speak with them "from above the mercy seat, from between the two cherubim which are on the ark of the Testimony, about everything which I will give you in commandment to the children of Israel" (Exod. 25:22).

Like the tabernacle, the High Priest is clothed in several layers, but the order is reversed. The most ordinary garments, such as the simple tunic, are closest to the priest's body, whereas in the tabernacle, the simplest materials are on the outside. Then come curtains of blue, purple, and scarlet, and finally, deep within, the Holy of Holies and the golden Ark. The priest wears blue, purple, and scarlet over the ordinary materials, and the golden breastplate in the most visible position of all.

Now we are in a position to understand fully why the High Priest wears the vestments of gold for the "outside service," when he appears before the people. In his own person he displays the Holy of Holies. He bears the image of God before the people. Within the Holy of Holies, he comes as a humble man seeking purification and forgiveness from sin. It would be inappropriate for him to enter the Holy of Holies wearing the adornment of the Holy of Holies. Before the people, however, he is dressed as the image-bearer of the divine glory.

The High Priest identifies with us all and represents us all. He can bear the image of the divine because all humans were created as divine image-bearers (Gen. 1:27). Further, by bearing the image of the Holy of Holies, he reveals the exalted assignment given to all humankind. We are made not only **in** God's image, but also **as** God's image, to represent God before all creation.

It is significant that our reading of this passage falls every year near Yom HaShoah, the day when we remember the devastation of the Holocaust. As we recall this ultimate desecration of the divine image in human beings, we need to also remember the glory for which God created us.

Honor Your Elders

Parashat K'doshim, Leviticus 19:1–20:27

In honor of my father Arnold E. Resnik, Aharon ben Shmu'el, August 13, 1915–April 10, 1999

Many of the instructions of Leviticus seem antiquated and inaccessible, so that they are not often studied today, and even less often carried out. True, some of these mitzvot relate to the temple worship and no longer directly apply to our behavior. Others are obscure or highly specialized. Yet, sadly, we ignore even some of the clearest ethical teachings in Leviticus. One example of this neglect is the commandment; "You shall rise up before the gray head and honor the presence of an old man, and fear your God. I am Adonai" (19:32). This instruction reflects the general concern of Torah for justice for the weak and disenfranchised.

Shortly after my father died at the age of 83, our local newspaper carried the story of some high school students, described by their teacher as "tough kids," who helped rebuild the dilapidated home of a 76-year-old woman confined to a wheelchair. One of the students, 16-year-old Pete Ramirez, described the experience: "It feels great. Maybe when I'm old and can't take care of my house, some kids will take care of me" (Albuquerque Journal, 4/22/99). Young Pete instinctively understood the community solidarity that Torah seeks to promote, a solidarity that demands proper respect for the aged.

When Leviticus commands us to honor our elders, however, it transcends even this essential concern for community. "You shall rise up before the gray head and honor the presence of an old man, and fear your God. I am Adonai" (19:32). The Lord links honoring the aged to the fear of God, and to his own name, punctuating this mitzvah with the statement, "I am Adonai." Here is an instruction about human life as God intends it to be lived. We are often reminded that we live in a "now society" that values the qualities of youth—looks, energy, spontaneity—over the qualities of age—experience, wisdom, endurance. Life as we moderns imagine it is a quick ascent through childhood and adolescence to the high point of young adulthood. Beyond those early years, we anticipate a slow but inexorable decline toward a lengthy middle age, and then the final years of old age. Since we imagine our destination in this way, we seek to avoid it through physical fitness, plastic surgery, and euphemisms. Old people are called (but not treated as) "honored citizens"; they often go off to "retirement centers," or "leisure villages," and thereby become isolated from the young, and from those who do not want to be reminded that they are no longer young.

Scripture, in contrast, presents the startling notion that human beings improve with age. The elderly may be physically weaker, and more likely to need assistance, than the young, but their age itself is worthy of honor. "You shall rise up before the gray head and honor the presence of an old man. . ."

The sages wondered if this mitzvah would apply even to the elderly who are "uncultivated." Modern philology traces the Hebrew root for "old man"—*zaken*—to *zakan*, meaning "beard." The elders are the bearded ones. Rashi, however, follows the early commentators who see *zaken* as derived from the root *kanah*, meaning to gain or acquire. In this view, the elders are the ones who have gained wisdom. The verse, "You shall rise up before the gray head and honor the presence of an old man. . ." instructs us to honor particularly that "gray head" who has become a *zaken* through acquiring the wisdom of Torah.

Ramban counters this view with that expressed in the Talmud (Kiddushin 32b):

> Scripture is commanding us [in the first half of the verse] to honor any old man, even the uncultured, that is the unlearned, and then [in the second half of the verse] it gives another commandment concerning the *zaken*, that is, one who has acquired wisdom, even if he be young and learned.

The aged are to be honored primarily for their wisdom and experience, and such qualities are to be honored in any person, even the young. Age itself, however, brings status and recognition. Here, as in many other passages, Torah is teaching that human life is precious, not because of its attributes such as physical appearance or strength, wealth, power, or even learning. Rather, human life has inherent worth, and those who have experienced more of it, who have weathered the threats and assaults against it, merit special honor.

The Sayings of the Fathers reflects the same perspective:

> Rabbi Yose bar Yehudah of Kfar ha-Bavli said, "He who learns from the young, what is he like? Like one who eats unripe grapes and drinks wine from his winepress. But he who learns from the old, what is he like? Like one who eats ripe grapes and drinks old wine."

> Rabbi said, "Do not look at the vessel, but what is in it; there is a new vessel filled with old wine and an old vessel that does not even contain new wine." (Pirke Avot 4:26–27)

Human beings, like wine, improve with age. According to Rabbi Yose, they become mellow, sweet, nourishing, like ripe grapes. Rabbi (probably Yehudah ha-Nasi, the redactor of the Mishnah) counters with the view that this is not necessarily so; sometimes the young have these same qualities of learning. Even his view, however, recognizes that normally we expect to find the fine old wine, the proven wisdom of Torah, in the old vessels. And, as the Messiah declares in a different context, "No one, having drunk old wine, desires the new; for he says, 'The old is better'" (Luke 15:39).

In commanding honor toward the elderly, Torah recasts the trajectory of human life. A life span is a steady ascent from innocent but untested youth, through the responsibility and growing influence of adulthood, to the final honor and prestige of old age. In the Scriptures, the elders sit in the gate of the city to rule the people. They do not spend their final years on the golf course or playing bridge, but in active engagement with their community, so that it can benefit from their experience and insight. Life as God designed it does not culminate in isolation and trivial activity, but in influence and connection.

Honor toward the elderly is right not only because it recognizes the value of experience and endurance, but because it frees us from the pressure of our fleeting youth. The modern view of life gives us a few precious years to capture life's pleasures and make our mark on the world before we begin our long decline. As a result we grow ever more hurried, driven, even ruthless, in pursuit of success. The Torah views life as a steady progression upward. Life does not reach its prime at thirty-five or forty, but at seventy or eighty. We can savor the journey, knowing we will continue to learn and grow as the years go by. One final point: Honor is tangible. The mitzvah instructs us to literally stand up when an older person enters the room. Rashi adds, "What is honor? One should not sit in an elder's place, nor should he speak in his place, nor should he contradict his words." Honor to the elderly compels us to learn from them, to slow down if necessary and listen to their stories and lessons, not in a condescending fashion, but to improve ourselves and our world.

Visible acts of deference and respect toward the elderly bind the community together. In a day of isolation and even hostility between the generations, this is an essential teaching.

Sanctification of the Name

Parashat Emor, Leviticus 21:1–24:23

> *Now an Israelite woman's son, whose father was an Egyptian, went out among the sons of Israel. And the Israelite woman's son and a man of Israel quarreled in the camp, and the Israelite woman's son blasphemed the Name, and cursed. And they brought him to Moses . . . and put him in custody, till the mind of the LORD should be declared to them.*

The sin of the Israelite woman's son is so significant that the Torah records the verdict against him, and even his execution for blaspheming the name of Adonai. Then in the verses following, the Torah outlines the law of "eye for eye and tooth for tooth" (24:20). This law is often misinterpreted as a call for vengeance, but actually it is a call for equity; the punishment must fit the crime. The sages generally did not apply it literally, but rather as a principle in deciding the proper penalty or fine for a crime. Perhaps this law is placed here to underline the seriousness of blaspheming the name of the Lord.

Why does the Torah consider this crime worthy of death? Israel is to bear witness to the name of Adonai. Blasphemy undermines this divine purpose and diminishes Israel's impact on the world around them.

Judaism teaches that certain sins—idolatry, incest, and murder—are so grievous that they disgrace the name of God. Generally, one is to set aside any commandment if necessary to preserve life, but to avoid these cardinal sins one must be willing even to give up one's life. Such a death is considered *Kiddush HaShem*, sanctification of the name. More commonly, though, sanctification of the name is the task of the living; to remain faithful to God and his laws even in the face of difficulty, opposition, and defeat. Just as the crime of blasphemy or disgracing the name was a public offense, so sanctification of the name is a public act of faith that testifies to the supremacy of God, often in the midst of unbelief and evil.

Job provides us with a prime example of Kiddush HaShem. He faced a similar temptation to that of the son of the Israelite woman; indeed, a much greater temptation. After Job loses everything he held dear, his children, his wealth, and his health, his wife counsels him to "Curse God and die." The son of the Israelite woman cursed God with little apparent provocation, in the heat of a fight. Job feels abandoned by God, punished although he is without sin. Surely, he has more reason to turn against God after everything has turned against him. Instead, he tells his wife, "'You speak as one of the foolish women speaks. Shall we indeed accept good from God, and shall we not accept adversity?' In all this Job did not sin with his lips" (Job 2:9–10). Indeed, in all this Job sanctified the name of God by remaining faithful to him in his afflictions.

Moreover, Job is an example not only of remaining faithful through suffering, but of remaining faithful through suffering that he does not deserve and cannot explain. The medieval rabbi and philosopher Saadiah Gaon, in his commentary on Job, shows that Job's sufferings had to remain unexplained. Normally in the Scriptures, when a character asks God why he is afflicted, Saadiah writes, "If the victim had suffered deservedly, God made it clear to him and told him, 'This is for your wrong doing.'" But when the righteous suffered, "God did not explain his sufferings, so as not to undermine his forbearance in people's eyes. . . . God does not directly inform them that they will be recompensed. Rather they must persevere on the basis of their reason alone" (The Book of Theodicy: Translation and Commentary on the Book of Job by Saadiah ben Joseph Al-Fayyumi, Chapter 38 [Yale Judaica Series XXV]).

We might write that they must persevere "on the basis of their faith alone" instead of "reason alone," but the point remains. Sometimes the sanctification of God's name requires suffering for no apparent cause. Kiddush HaShem is a public act of faith before an unbelieving world. The perseverance of the righteous testifies publicly that God is worthy of our love in all circumstances, that his grace alone is sufficient in all trials. If God's people love and serve him even without visible reward, he must be a great God indeed.

Saadiah continues, "Job was being tested. His detractors before God [Satan the adversary and his cohorts] were particularly not to be given the opening to say that it was only because he had been assured of his future recompense that he endured, as one has the fortitude to drink a medicine when told that it will do him good." Job is assured of recompense in the resurrection, of course, but he does not know the reason or the outcome of his sufferings in this world. He endures not just to get a reward, but because he knows that God is worthy of his trust even in the midst of suffering. Hence, his remarkable perseverance testifies not only to Job's faithfulness, but to the transcendent goodness of God. It is a sanctification of the name.

Shimon in the New Covenant scriptures also speaks of the sanctification of the name. He tells servants to serve faithfully, even if they are treated unfairly. If this instruction applied to slaves in Shimon's day, how much more will it apply to us who are free!

> But when you do good and suffer, if you take it patiently, this is commendable before God. For to this you were called, because Messiah also suffered for us, leaving us an example, that you should follow his steps: "Who committed no sin, nor was deceit found in his mouth"; who, when he was reviled, did not revile in return; when he suffered, he did not threaten, but committed himself to him who judges righteously; who himself bore our sins in his own body on the tree, that we, having died to sins, might live for righteousness—by whose stripes you were healed. (1 Pet. 2:20–24, NKJV)

Like Saadiah, Shimon commends the suffering of the righteous. Such suffering is mysterious and we can dishonor it by trying to provide reasons or consolations of our own devising. This was the failure of Job's friends; they sought to explain Job's sufferings according to their own dogmas, and in the end God was angry with them, because they had not spoken rightly (Job 42:7). We, too, must guard against our tendency to explain the suffering of the innocent, or worse, to find a reason to blame them for it.

Accordingly, Shimon does not attempt to explain our suffering, but he does point to an example. Messiah himself accepted undeserved suffering without complaint, and this suffering was the greatest sanctification of the name. Those who suffer in Messiah need not ask, "Why me?" Instead, they learn to follow a Messiah who also suffered, even to the point of death by torture and separation from God. Peter portrays this acceptance of undeserved suffering as an aspect of our restoration to God: "For you were like sheep going astray, but have now returned to the Shepherd and Overseer of your souls" (2:25, NKJV).

Sanctification of the name sometimes requires that we abandon our rights, advancement, and convenience to simply remain faithful to God and his word. Despite our expectations, such sacrifice may bring no visible reward. Suffering cannot always be explained or ameliorated, but it may speak to others, as nothing else can, of the reality of our God. "Live such good lives among the pagans that, though they accuse you of doing wrong, they may see your good deeds and glorify God on the day he visits us" (1 Pet. 2:12).

The Great Shofar

Parashat B'har, Leviticus 25:1–26:2

Two themes dominate the final chapters of Leviticus: the laws of the sabbatical year and Jubilee, and the prediction of Israel's exile and eventual restoration. These two themes, though apparently quite distinct, are in fact intimately related.

The sabbatical year ordinance (25:1–8) requires that the Israelites give their land a rest every seven years. Farmers are neither to sow nor harvest during the seventh year. All the inhabitants of the land are free to eat whatever grows of itself in any field, but they are not to work the field in any way, or to use the food for commerce.

Moses goes on to instruct the people to count off seven cycles of sabbatical years, or a total of forty-nine years. Then on Yom Kippur at the beginning of the fiftieth year they are to sound the shofar to signal the year of Jubilee, "and proclaim freedom throughout the land for all its inhabitants. . . . Each of you shall return to his holding and each of you shall return to his family" (25:10). The Jubilee is a year of rest for the land, like the sabbatical years, but it also is a year of return or restoration. Any land holding that has been sold in Israel reverts back to its original owners; it is restored to the family inheritance. Any Israelite who has sold himself into slavery is set free so that he can "return to his family." Jubilee restores the original order of Israel as Adonai intended it to be.

Jubilee in Hebrew is *yoveil,* a word generally taken to mean "the ram's horn," referring to the shofar that is blown to inaugurate the fiftieth year. Ramban, however, objects; "What sense is there in saying of a year that 'it shall be "a blowing" to you' and you shall return'?" Further, he points out that the shofar need not necessarily be a ram's horn, but can be made of the horn of the wild goat. Following Ibn Ezra, Ramban sees the word yoveil as meaning "sending forth" or "bringing" the liberty that characterizes the year.

Thus the meaning of *it shall be 'yoveil' to you* is "it is a year that brings liberty and it shall be so to all of you, that you shall come *and return every man to his holding, and every man to his family."* And he stated again, *A 'yoveil' shall that fiftieth year be to you,* meaning that the fiftieth year shall be to you only for yoveil [bringing liberty], and not for anything else, and *you shall not sow, neither reap,* but instead it *shall be holy . . .*

This liberty, as the Lord explains it, has profound significance: "The land shall not be sold in perpetuity, for the land is mine, for you are strangers and sojourners with me" (25:23), and "the children of Israel are servants to me; they are my servants, whom I have taken out of the land of Egypt—I am Adonai your God" (25:55). The Jubilee marks the Lord's possession of the land and people of Israel; nothing belongs to them but to the Lord alone. Yet, remarkably, this status as the possession of the Lord makes the people free, and the Jubilee is the year of freedom.

After giving these laws, Moses predicts that the Israelites will wander from Torah and receive God's punishment; sickness, famine, defeat in war, and eventually exile from the land. Specifically Israel will be exiled for neglecting the law of the sabbatical year. Thus, according to Rashi, Israel ignored seventy sabbatical years from its earliest times in the land until the destruction of the first temple. Hence the exile lasted seventy years to make up for the neglected sabbaticals.

Then the land will enjoy its sabbaticals during all the years of its desolation, while you are in the land of your foes. Then the land will rest and will enjoy its sabbaticals. All the years of its desolation it will rest, for the time it did not rest during your sabbaticals when you dwelt upon it. (26:34–35)

The exile results in part from the broken laws of sabbatical and Jubilee, but these same laws determine that the exile will not go on forever, but must end in restoration. Each Israelite returns to his ancestral inheritance and to his family in the year of Jubilee, to demonstrate that they and the Land belong to the Lord alone; no one else may take final possession of them. In the same way all Israel belongs to the Lord alone, not to the nations, nor to secular history, and must in the end return to its ancestral inheritance. "But despite all this [Israel's sin and exile], when they are in the land of their enemies I will not cast them away, nor will I reject them to utterly destroy them (26:44–45)

Toward the end of this predicted exile, Daniel the prophet sees that the seventy years—corresponding to the seventy neglected sabbaticals—are nearly completed, and begins to intercede for Israel's restoration. The Lord shows him that another series of seventy sabbaticals, literally seventy "sevens," lies ahead, "To finish the transgression, to make an end of sins, to make reconciliation for iniquity, to bring in everlasting righteousness, to seal up vision and prophecy, and to anoint the Most Holy" (Dan. 9:24).

Only the Sanhedrin in the days of the temple had authority to keep the count of the year of Jubilee, so that this is one of the laws of Torah that cannot be fulfilled until all is restored. The Lord himself, however, decrees a final Jubilee that will come to pass in the last days, a Jubilee that will herald the restoration of all things, and especially the restoration of Israel. A prayer in the Shemoneh Esreh, or Eighteen Benedictions of the Hebrew prayer book, takes up the imagery of Jubilee to describe the promised redemption: "Sound the great shofar for our freedom, and raise a banner to gather our exiles, and gather us together from the four corners of the earth. Blessed are you O Lord who gathers in the exiles of his people Israel."

As on Yom Kippur of the year of Jubilee, the sound of the shofar calls each one back to his inheritance and back to his family; Israel in physical and spiritual exile is called back to its land, to its people, and to its Father, Adonai. The opening line of this prayer is adapted from Isaiah 11:12. The prophet takes up Jubilee imagery again in 61:1–2:

> The spirit of the Lord Adonai is upon me, because Adonai has anointed me to announce good tidings to the meek. He has sent me to bind up the broken hearted, to proclaim liberty to the captives, and the opening of the prison to them that are bound; to proclaim an acceptable year of Adonai, and a day of vengeance of our God.

These verses are, of course, the ones that Yeshua read in his home synagogue in Nazareth, saying "Today this Scripture is fulfilled in your hearing" (Luke 4:18–21). Significantly, he left off the last phrase, "a day of vengeance of our God." Yeshua was sounding the shofar of a Jubilee to begin with his work in Galilee, restoring the captives of Israel in that day, the poor, the sick, the outcast, to their inheritance and families. This was not the final Jubilee foretold in Torah, which will also be a day of God's justice upon the ungodly. Rather, Yeshua in himself embodied, and still embodies, the Jubilee to come. The good tidings of Messiah are a foretaste of the proclamation of good tidings that will take place at the final sounding of the shofar. For those who will not hear, it will be "a day of vengeance of our God."

The Nazareth townsfolk were not ready to receive Yeshua's words, but God's purposes for them, and for all Israel, remain unchanged. Israel is God's possession, and the Jubilee must come when it returns to its inheritance; the history of all nations will culminate in the day of messianic restoration for Israel.

The Reward of Obedience

Parashat B'chukkotai, Leviticus 26:3–27:34

If you walk in My statutes, and keep My command-
ments, and do them, then I will give your rains in
their season, and the land shall yield her produce,
and the trees of the field shall yield their fruit. (Lev.
26:3–4)

The Lord graciously promises the Israelites a visible reward for obedience, but this promise presents an unexpected difficulty. The sages of the Mishnah, and many Jewish thinkers after them, teach that we are not to obey the divine instruction for the sake of reward, nor to expect a reward, especially in this world.

The Mishnah, of course, was compiled a generation or two after the defeat of Bar Kochba, and the crushing of Jewish hope for independence from Rome. Memories of persecution under the emperor Hadrian were still fresh in the minds of the rabbis. Even the earlier sages, who taught long before the fall of Jerusalem, lived under the shadow of foreign domination, and with the memory of Antiochus and his desecration of the Temple.

Those who were most faithful to Torah in those days received beatings, exile, and death, not a reward from above. The sages speak well to our modern age, which also has trouble expecting a visible reward for those who seek to follow God's ways. Perhaps they made a virtue of necessity—since no reward was forthcoming in this life, we should not seek one at all.

Antigonus of Socho . . . used to say: Be not like servants who serve their master for the sake of receiving a reward. Rather, be like servants who serve their master not for the sake of receiving a reward. And let the fear of Heaven be upon you. (Pirke Avot 1:3)

Rabbi Tarfon assured students of Torah that they would indeed be rewarded, but reminded them that "the reward of the righteous will be given in the age to come" (Pirke Avot 2.21). Rabbi Tzadok went further. He quotes Hillel's saying—"He who exploits the crown [of Torah] shall fade away"—and adds: "Whoever exploits the words of Torah removes his life from this world" (Pirke Avot 4.7). By this it was understood that one should gain no advantage, and should certainly not earn one's living, from teaching Torah. Hillel was the example. The greatest sage of his time, and one of the great luminaries of Jewish history, he supported himself as a poor woodchopper his whole life.

Yeshua teaches to the same effect:

> Which of you, having a servant plowing or tending sheep, will say to him when he has come in from the field, "Come at once and sit down to eat"? But will he not rather say to him, "Prepare something for my supper, and gird yourself and serve me till I have eaten and drunk, and afterward you will eat and drink"? Does he thank that servant because he did the things that were commanded him? I think not. So likewise you, when you have done all those things which you are commanded, say, "We are unprofitable servants. We have done what was our duty to do." (Luke 17:7–10, NKJV)

In seeming contrast to all this, the Lord in our passage promises Israel ample reward **in this world** for observing Torah. He will invite them to "come at once and sit down to eat" as the Land produces grain and fruit in abundance. Moreover, he seems to use this promise to motivate Israel to obedience, just as he uses the threat of exile in the following verses to warn them against disobedience.

Jewish tradition places great value on study of Torah *lishma*—for its own sake—without thought of any reward apart from the reward of study itself. But that is not the tone that is set in the closing arguments of Leviticus.

The Sefat Emet grapples with this problem in his commentary on this parasha:

> Even though the sages taught that there is no reward in this world for fulfilling the commandments, that is true only rationally and from our human point of view. But in fact, God has made the law of the entire universe depend upon Torah.

Since it is taught that the world was created through Torah, the connection between world and Torah is higher than the rational mind [can reach]. But a person who transcends his own self, truly "following His laws," is given sustenance by Torah in this world as well.

When Sefat Emet speaks of "the rational mind," he may be referring to a cold and calculating approach to the service of God. The one who expects a strict equivalency between his efforts in obedience and the God-given reward will be—and *should be*—disappointed. He is making merchandise of his obedience to Torah, demanding that a certain degree of effort be compensated with a certain degree of reward from on high. Such an attitude is only "rational" and "human" and cannot recognize the gracious purposes of God.

The one who serves Torah for its own sake, however, will indeed discover rewards in this age, as well as in the age to come. Like the servants in Yeshua's story, we are to serve the Lord because that is our duty, without expecting great recognition for our service. Yet, once we break with any sense of merchandising in our obedience to the Lord, we discover that there is a great return.

The one who would exploit the crown of Torah in Hillel's sense is seeking human reward, such as recognition or income, from the divine gift. This is a betrayal. We are to serve God because it is an honor to do so, because it elevates our souls and our lives, not because we hope for recognition from others. Yet, such service expresses a cooperation with the divine purpose that may well bring great blessing into our lives.

Yeshua captured this distinction well.

And when you pray, you shall not be like the hypocrites. For they love to pray standing in the synagogues and on the corners of the streets, *that they may be seen by men*. Assuredly, I say to you, *they have their reward*. But you, when you pray, go into your room, and when you have shut your door, pray to your Father who is in the secret place; and your Father who sees in secret will *reward you openly*. (Matt. 6:5–6, NKJV; emphasis mine)

Loving dedication to the Lord and his ways discovers a reward that more calculating service cannot imagine. A divine reward awaits those who renounce human reward.

במדבר
The Book of Numbers

Numbers is set entirely in the wilderness, telling of Israel's journeys over 38 years from Mount Sinai to the Plains of Moab just across the Jordan from Jericho. Accordingly the name of the book in Hebrew is B'midbar, "in the wilderness."

The wilderness is the scene of Israel's wanderings, both physically and spiritually, and Numbers traces several complaints and rebellions against God and Moses, culminating in Israel's refusal to enter the Promised Land. The penalty is that the generation that refused to enter the Promised Land will die in the wilderness. The wanderings will continue for a total of forty years, most of which are covered in this book.

Paradoxically, though, the wilderness is also the scene of Israel's maturing. Israel begins to win battles; they defeat Sihon and Og, and apparently are being blessed by God. These victories strike fear in the heart of Israel's enemies, and particularly Balak, the King of Moab, who hires Balaam the prophet to curse Israel. Instead, he must bless them, because despite outward appearances and behavior, they remain God's chosen people. Even after a final outbreak of rebellion, the worship of God is restored and Israel is brought back to God's blessing.

This seems to be the theme of the whole book. Israel must wander in the wilderness because of its unbelief, yet here it is prepared to fulfill its destiny. God's purpose in bringing Israel forth from Egypt will be accomplished. Before the book concludes, Joshua will be raised up as the leader of the new generation, and the Land is divided between the twelve tribes.

Interwoven with this narrative are a number of sections of legal and ritual interest. The book opens with a genealogy of the generation of the wilderness (hence, its title "Numbers"), and includes a genealogy of the generation that will enter the Promised Land in its final chapters. Sections of legal instruction alternate with the great dramatic narratives of rebellion and restoration. Translator

Everett Fox notes that, while there are outward obstacles to be overcome in the wilderness, "the main emphasis in these texts is on internal obstacles—the people's lack of trust, faith, and courage. And as so often happens in the Torah, physical background, as important as it obviously is in Numbers, what with a myriad of geographical locations noted, is overshadowed by the dominant issue of the relationship between Israel and God."[1]

Order in the Wilderness

Parashat B'midbar, Numbers 1:1–4:20

Some of my neo-Pentecostal friends are fond of the slogan, "We have to get out of the Book of Numbers and into the Book of Acts." By this they mean that congregations should worry less about numerical and financial growth and more about spiritual impact. A valid enough concern, but it misses the point of the numbering in the Book of Numbers. It is God who orders Moses to count the Israelites: "Take a census of all the congregation of the sons of Israel, according to families, according to fathers' houses, by the number of the names, every male, head by head, from twenty years old and up, all in Israel who are able to go forth to war" (Num. 1:2–3).

The Hebrew name of Numbers—and of our current parasha—unlocks the meaning of this census. *B'midbar* means "in the wilderness." This is the setting for the Lord's instruction to number the sons of Israel. Wilderness in the Torah is a place hostile to humankind, "that great and terrible wilderness, in which were fiery serpents and scorpions and thirsty land where there was no water . . ." (Deut. 8:15).

Wilderness is the place of Israel's wanderings, and B'midbar is the book of wandering. In the middle of the book twelve spies are sent out to survey the promised land. They return with a majority report that discourages the people from entering the land and results in the forty years of wandering. Not only is the wilderness a hostile place, it is the place where Israel must remain because of its failure to respond to God's purpose.

This, then, is the setting of the divinely ordered census. When the Lord commands Moses to number the people, he is granting him a new perspective on the whole matter. Human eyes see a dry and fruitless land and a miserable band wandering in it. The census imposes order and dignity upon this scene. Israel may look (and act) like a collection of scarcely freed slaves, but they are numbered as ranks of fighting men who will encamp in strict order around the tabernacle of meeting.

Numbering, like naming, implies mastery, control, a sense of purpose. The information revolution, the great technological accomplishment of the late twentieth century, reflects this same reality. It proceeds by reducing information to a digital code, in effect numbering everything. In the midst of the modern collapse of values and absolute meaning, we have regained a sense of control through numbers. Life may look like a wilderness, but we have tamed it digitally.

Such numbering, however, does not in itself change anything; rather it transforms our perspective. It gives us a way to manage and manipulate what is already there.

What seems to be a similar transformation of perspective occurs later in B'midbar in the story of Balaam the prophet. The enemies of Israel feel threatened by these wanderers, but are confident that they can readily dispose of them with a proper curse. Balaam, hired to curse Israel, sets his face toward the wilderness and raises his eyes to look upon Israel, but when the Spirit of God comes upon him he can only pronounce a blessing:

> How lovely are your tents, O Jacob! Your dwellings, O Israel!
> Like valleys that stretch out, like gardens by the riverside,
> Like aloes planted by the LORD, like cedars beside the waters.
> (24:5–6, NKJV)

As with Moses's census, prophetic vision transforms the wilderness rabble into ranks of order and fruitfulness, into a garden. But we moderns may become confused here. Is Israel *really* a fruitful garden, or is it really a band of wanderers? Is the message of Torah that we have the power to impose order upon the chaos and relativism of human existence, that everything depends upon one's perspective?

Such an idea was eloquently put forth by Argentine author Tomas Eloy Martinez in his recent novel *Santa Evita*:

> Was *Santa Evita* going to be a novel? I didn't know and I didn't care. Story lines, fixed points of view, the laws of space and times, slipped through my fingers. The characters

sometimes spoke in their own voices and sometimes in other people's, merely to explain to me that history is not always historical, that the truth is never what it appears to be. It took me months and months to tame the chaos. . . . Every story is, by definition, unfaithful. Reality, as I've said, can't be told or repeated. The only thing that can be done with reality is to invent it again.

So is the census simply a way to re-invent reality? Is the prophet's perspective just another way of looking at things? Such a message would certainly be palatable to today's reader, but hardly reflects the genius of Torah.

Ramban provides a clue to this issue. In his commentary on B'midbar, he struggles with the fact that God commands a census here, but later punishes King David for taking a census. Ramban theorizes that God became angry with David because he counted Israel "unnecessarily . . . only to make him rejoice that he ruled over a large people." He cites the Midrash (Bemidbar Rabbah 2:17):

Whenever Israel was counted for a purpose, their numbers did not diminish, but when they were counted for no purpose, they became diminished. When were they counted for a purpose? In the days of Moses, for the setting up of the standards and the division of the Land. When were they counted for no purpose? In the days of David.

In the divine perspective, David's selfish purpose is no purpose. The divine purpose is not just another way of looking at things, of inventing reality again. Rather, it is the one purpose that delivers us from our self-centered perspective into genuine meaning. When Moses numbers Israel, or when Balaam prophesies, they are not simply imposing a grid upon what is really chaos, but are revealing the genuine order that the chaos obscures.

Balaam gets the final word. After he looks past the wilderness to see Israel as a garden, he describes himself as "the man whose eyes are opened . . . who falls down with eyes wide open" (24:15, 16). Our task is not to create order within the chaos, but to discover it.

This article first appeared in the Summer '99 edition of Boundaries. *Used by permission.*

God our Keeper

Parashat Naso, Numbers 4:21–7:89

Ten or twelve years ago an archaeology team from Tel Aviv University excavated an ancient tomb in Jerusalem that had been used by a family over many generations. Among the finds were two tiny amulets, little strips of silver an inch or so wide and three to four inches long, rolled up into a tube to be worn on a string around the neck. Archaeologists took three years to unroll the silver tubes, to give the metal time to adjust without shattering. They found letters inscribed on the silver that dated from before the destruction of the first temple, around 600 BCE, spelling out the words,

> The Lord bless you and keep you.
> The Lord make his face to shine upon you and be gracious to you.
> The Lord lift up his face to you and give you shalom—peace.

These words are, of course, Numbers 6:24–26, the *birkat kohanim* or priestly blessing from this week's parasha. When they were discovered they became by about 400 years the oldest written fragment of the Bible that we possess. It is not surprising that an ancient Israelite would choose these verses to preserve on silver and wear around the neck, because the Torah says that these are the words by which the Lord will bless the children of Israel.

What is a blessing? It is a word of favor, affirmation, and power, given by a father or one in authority, or by God himself, to one subject to him. Torah teaches that a word is not just a sound or an utterance, but that it has inherent power. The blessing gives us power and direction for life, and its lack—or perceived lack—is the source of all kinds of social and personal ills.

God blesses humankind beginning with Adam, then Noah, Abraham and his sons, and now finally in the Book of Numbers all the children of Israel. They have received Torah, built the tabernacle, begun the worship of God, taken a census of all the people, and now are ready to leave Sinai. God blesses his chosen people Israel as they are about to step onto the stage of human history.

The blessing that the Lord commands is fitting for an amulet, for it is like a jewel in its perfection and artfulness. It consists of three lines, each containing the name Adonai, and each invoking a paired blessing, for a total of six blessings. In the original Hebrew, each line is longer than the preceding one; the first is three words, the second five words, and the third seven words. Adonai is the source of blessing that expands until it culminates in the word Shalom, a word that expresses the full intention of the God of Israel toward his people. The blessing is multiplied six-fold, and the seventh is this: "So they shall put my name on the children of Israel, and I will bless them" (6:27). Adonai links the blessing inextricably to his own name.

Through the blessing God's name is placed upon Israel. He is the God of blessing and his people are distinguished by the blessing that rests upon them. The blessing, however, is complex. Its first line is *y'varechecha Adonai v'yishmarecha*, "The Lord bless you and keep you." These opening words define the entire blessing, and bring out an aspect of blessing we might easily overlook: being kept or guarded by God.

The Hebrew root for "keep"—*shamar*—appears often throughout Torah. We are to keep or guard the commandments of the Lord, to keep the ordinance of the tabernacle, to keep Shabbat. The Psalmist tells us that the Lord keeps or guards Israel collectively, and that he keeps the individual Israelite who trusts in him. It is in the word's first appearance in Torah, however, that we learn its real significance within the priestly blessing.

In the beginning the Lord places Adam in the Garden of Eden and commands him "to work it and to keep it" (Gen 2:15; *l'avdah ul'shamrah*). To work the garden means to tend and maintain it. To keep or guard it implies that there is an outside threat from which the garden must be protected. When we keep the commandments, we do so in the context of pressures to disobey, to go our own way. Instead we guard God's way. When we keep Shabbat, we guard it against the pressures to treat it like one of the ordinary days of the week. Likewise God charges Adam to guard the garden knowing that temptation and sin will soon enter in. When Adam fails to keep the garden he and the woman, Eve, are cast out. Then the word *shamar* appears a second time in the Eden story. "So God drove out the man, and he placed cherubim at the east of the garden of Eden, and a flaming sword which turned every way, to **guard** the way to the tree of life" (3:24).

Because Adam failed to guard the garden, the Lord guards the garden from him. Guarding keeps us within the parameters of blessing. Thus the kohen says, "May the Lord bless you and keep you in a condition to receive blessing. May his blessing not be a passing experience, but an abiding condition of obedience and right standing with the Lord." In the first paired blessing, the Lord provides the blessing itself and also the promise to keep his children within the parameters of blessing. This promise involves both protection and discipline, helping us to keep out of our lives all that would disqualify us for blessing. Thus, the Midrash asks, "What is the meaning of the expression 'keep you'? From the Evil Inclination, that he not drive you out of the world" (Bemidbar Rabbah 11:5). God protects us from many things, including our own tendency to evil and rebellion.

The authority to bless carries also the authority to protect, chastise, and discipline. The risen Messiah, who claims identity with the God of Israel, sends a warning to a wayward congregation: "As many as I love I rebuke and chasten; be zealous therefore and return to me" (Rev. 3:19). He links his love, the unqualified and abundant **blessing**, with the chastisement that **keeps** us from wandering off from the blessing.

The God of Israel is benevolent but not insipid. We are simplistic when we imagine a deity whose blessing requires no discipline, who expects only a passive response from humankind. Adonai freely blesses, but he also makes demands upon his people, and they cannot have the blessing without responding to these demands. Indeed, this truth can be said to characterize the God of Israel and distinguish him from all false concepts of God.

May the Lord bless you and keep you safe from everything that would diminish his blessing . . . including your own tendency to wander from his will.

Torah and Spirit

Parashat B'ha'alotkha, Numbers 8:1–12:16

*Ben Bag Bag says: Turn it (the Torah) and turn it
again, for all things are contained within it . . .*
(Pirke Avot 5:22)

The Torah contains all things, even things that seem to transcend
its own rules and ordinances. Thus, in last week's parasha, after the
LORD has brought Israel out of Egypt, given them laws and ordinances, tabernacle and priesthood, Shabbat and festivals, and declared them to be a kingdom of priests and a holy nation, he makes
provision for the Nazir. Any Israelite, man or woman, who longs
for greater devotion to God may take on a voluntary vow of separation. Significantly, the rules of the Nazir require no reason for this
vow. They do not speculate why someone who is part of God's
segullah, his special treasure among all the nations, would seek
greater consecration. Rather they make provision, after all the rest
of the ordinances of holiness have been provided, for those who
simply desire more.

Likewise in this week's parasha, we see the hint of a spiritual life
beyond the specific definitions of Torah, a hint that fulfills Ben Bag
Bag's saying, "All things are contained within it."

In B'ha'alotkha, Israel finally begins its journey from Mount
Sinai towards the Promised Land. But after only a three-day journey from Sinai the people begin to complain, so that the LORD
sends fire upon them as chastisement. Immediately afterwards,
"the rabble" stirs up more complaints, this time about the meager
food of the wilderness. Moses hears the complaining of the people
and himself lodges a complaint against the LORD: "Why have you
done evil against your servant? Why have I not found favor in your

eyes, that you have laid the burden of this entire people upon me? I cannot bear this entire nation alone, for it is too heavy for me!" (Num. 11:11–14).

In response, the LORD shows Moses that he is not alone. He instructs him to gather seventy of the elders of Israel and stand with them at the Tent of Meeting. There, the LORD says, "I will take some of the spirit that is upon you and place it upon them, and they shall bear the burden of the people that is with you, and you shall not bear it alone" (11:16–17).

This wording suggests that the elders will not receive their own share of the spirit, but that Moses will now have to divide his portion among them. Thus the Midrash compares Moses to a caretaker of an orchard, who says to his master, "I cannot look after the whole of it." The master replies,

> I gave you the entire orchard to watch, handing to you all the fruits resulting from your care of it, and now you say: "Bring me additional men to help me watch!" I will bring you additional men, but I will not pay them wages for watching from my own funds but they will receive their wages from the payment that I have been giving to you!" (Numbers Rabbah 15:25)

Likewise, says the Midrash, God says to Moses, "'The seventy elders will receive nothing of mine, but *I will take of the Spirit that is upon you*' (Num. 11:17). This notwithstanding Moses lost nothing . . ." (Ibid.). As Yochanan writes in the New Covenant (John 3:34), "God does not give the spirit by measure." Moses's share is divided among the seventy, yet Moses is not diminished.

Like the ordinance for the Nazir, the widespread gift of the spirit is contained within Torah, yet is outside the normal bounds of Torah. In the book of the prophet Amos, the LORD links the Nazir and the prophet:

> "I raised up some of your sons as prophets,
> And some of your young men as Nazirites.
> Is it not so, O you children of Israel?"
> Says the LORD.
> "But you gave the Nazirites wine to drink,
> And commanded the prophets saying,
> 'Do not prophesy!'" (Amos 2:11–12, NKJV)

Prophets and Nazirites are special gifts to Israel whom God raises up. The Nazirite takes his vow voluntarily, but God raises him up by instilling the desire for greater devotion and providing the means to accomplish it. God raises up the prophet through the bestowal of his spirit. Both individuals point to a reality beyond the established religion of Torah, a reality of which Torah also speaks, and for which it yearns. In Amos' day, however, the people are content with just the externals, the status quo, and desire nothing more.

Not so Moses. The gift of prophecy begins to abound and two men who did not go out to the Tent of Meeting with Moses begin to prophesy in the camp. When Joshua urges Moses to forbid them, he replies, "Are you zealous for my sake? Would that all the LORD's people were prophets and that the Lord would put his spirit upon them!" (11:29)

Here in one statement is true spiritual greatness and profound prophetic insight. The commentators adduce a number of reasons why Joshua wanted to stop the two prophets, but the simplest reason is that they are under the authority of the master prophet, Moses, and should have spoken only with his permission. Moses is above such personal concerns; he is not interested in maintaining his status, but in magnifying the spirit of God among Israel. The two men may have violated the rules by prophesying in the wrong place or manner, but Moses recognizes that something greater is going on. With prophetic insight, he longs for a day when all Israel—not just the seventy elders—will receive the gift of the spirit. Thus, the Midrash concludes its commentary on this passage:

> The Holy One, blessed be he, said: "In Olam Hazeh, this age, only a few individuals have prophesied, but in Olam Haba, the age to come, all Israel will be made prophets," as it says, *And it shall come to pass afterward, that I will pour out my spirit upon all flesh, and your sons and your daughters shall prophesy, your old men,* etc. (Joel 3:1)

The Torah contains all things, even the things of the age to come. The outpouring of the spirit is the hallmark of the age to come, and the credentials of Messiah who inaugurates that age. After Yeshua's death and resurrection his disciples gathered in the

Temple courts to celebrate Shavuot. The spirit came upon them and they began to speak as the spirit empowered them. The crowd of worshipers demanded that the disciples explain their strange behavior. Peter, like the Midrash, quoted Joel's prophecy of the outpouring of the spirit, and told the crowd that the resurrected Messiah had "poured out this that you now see and hear" (Acts 2:33). The conclusion was inevitable: "Let all the house of Israel know assuredly that God has made this Yeshua, whom you crucified, both Lord and Messiah" (Acts 2:36, NKJV).

Moses' prophetic longing for Israel was fulfilled. Today we remain in Olam Hazeh, this age, but we taste the realities of the Age to Come in the gift of the spirit. Would that all the LORD's people were prophets and that the LORD would put his spirit upon them!

A Different Spirit

Parashat Shlach L'kha, Numbers 13:1–15:41

In the account of the twelve spies in this week's parasha, the Torah gives us a classic formulation of faith and doubt. One leading man from each tribe is chosen for the mission of spying out the Promised Land before the actual conquest begins. The mission will end in disaster when the spies return with a discouraging report and the people refuse to enter the land, even though two of the spies, Joshua and Caleb, assure them that they can conquer it. The Lord decrees that the entire generation that heeded the evil report will indeed never enter the land, but will die in the wilderness.

This ill-fated mission was not necessarily wrong in itself, but the story opens with a phrase that hints at trouble ahead. Adonai says to Moses, "*Shlach L'kha* [literally, send for yourself] men to spy out the land of Canaan" (Num. 13:2). Apparently, the LORD is not entirely sold on the idea of a reconnoitering mission. We learn from the parallel account in the first chapter of Deuteronomy that the people initiated the idea and Moses supported it. At some point the LORD added his reluctant endorsement and said, "Send for yourself the men."

Nonetheless, it was still not wrong to send a party to scout out the land in advance of the conquest. Because of a failure of nerve, however, the party changed their assignment. Now they were spying out the land to see *if* they should proceed with the conquest at all. Here is a contrast between faith and doubt. God commands the conquest. Faith assumes that the land will be conquered and seeks the way to accomplish it. Doubt assumes the land cannot be conquered unless convinced otherwise.

Before the spies go out, Moses gives them their assignment:

See what the land is like: whether the people who dwell in it
are strong or weak, few or many; whether the land they dwell
in is good or bad; whether the cities they inhabit are like
camps or strongholds; whether the land is rich or poor; and
whether there are forests there or not. Be of good courage.
And bring some of the fruit of the land. (13:18–20, NKJV)

The spies return with some of the fruit of the land and begin
their report. "We went to the land where you sent us. It truly flows
with milk and honey, and this is its fruit" (13:27). The spies might
have continued their report by simply describing the inhabitants
and cities as Moses had requested. Instead, they added one word of
strong negation, "Nevertheless,"—*ephes* in the Hebrew—before
continuing: "Nevertheless, the people who dwell in the land are
strong; the cities are fortified and very large; moreover we saw the
descendants of Anak there" (13:28).

The one word *ephes* spells the difference between faith and
doubt. All the spies saw the same realities in the land, but with this
one word, the majority recast their report into a prediction of defeat. Only Caleb and Joshua continued to insist that the Israelites
could conquer the land.

How fine is the line between faith and doubt! They see the
same realities, but interpret them far differently. Thus we read of
Abraham, that when God promised him a son,

He did not consider his own body, already dead (since he
was about a hundred years old), and the deadness of Sarah's
womb. He did not waver at the promise of God through
unbelief, but was strengthened in faith, giving glory to
God, and being fully convinced that what he had promised
he was also able to perform. (Rom. 4:19–20, NKJV)

The patriarch is confronted by the facts of his age and his wife's bar-
renness, but he does not "consider" these facts. He does not pretend
that they are untrue; he simply turns his attention to the divine
promise, and the character of the one who made the promise.

We learn from Abraham that faith gives glory to God; it en-
hances his reputation. Doubt, in contrast, is a slander against
God's reputation. Thus, the Midrash notes that the ten spies begin

their report well and then speak evil. "Such is the way of those who utter slander; they begin by speaking well of one and conclude by speaking ill" (Numbers Rabbah 16:17). The men were able to spy out the whole land, says the Midrash, because when they would enter a city, its leaders would be killed by a pestilence. The towns-people became so busy burying them that the spies were free to come and go. Yet, when they reported to the people they said only that the land consumed its inhabitants. "They used the miracles which the Holy One, blessed be he, wrought for them to spread slander" (ibid., 16:13).

Faith confronts the same circumstances as unbelief, but interprets them differently. Unbelief, like slander, takes an aspect of truth and develops it toward an evil purpose. Faith takes the same fragment of truth and views it in context of God's revealed purposes, convinced that what he promises he is also able to perform.

Not only do faith and doubt confront the same circumstances, but they both require . . . faith! When the Israelites hear the bad report and decide not to enter the Promised Land, they say "Let us select a leader and return to Egypt" (Num. 14:4). After all they endured to get as far as they have, this seems like a rather daring idea. Furthermore, after the Lord tells them they will not be allowed to enter the Promised Land, the people undergo what appears to be a superficial repentance, and then decide on their own to launch the conquest, even without the ark of the covenant or Moses—a bold move that ends in disaster.

Faith and doubt do not seem so far apart. Both begin with the same information and both can require bold action. So, what is the difference? The Lord says of Caleb that he has a different spirit (14:24). He is subject to the same limitations as the rest of the spies, the same fears and temptations, but he is animated by something different, a desire to follow God fully. Such a desire will find a way, despite the obstacles.

When Moses sent the spies out, he instructed them, "Be of good courage" (13:20). This phrase will become the motto of the conquest in the books of Deuteronomy and Joshua. We all know that courage is not the absence of fear, but the ability to do what needs to be done despite the fears, which are often entirely realistic. Joshua and Caleb recognize the obstacles to the Promised Land, but they choose to look past them. When they do, they see something the other spies miss, saying, "Do not fear the people of the land, for they are our bread; their shadow has departed from them, and the Lord is with us. Do not fear them" (14:9).

"Their shadow" refers to the protective covering provided by the pagan gods the Canaanites worshiped, which were actually demonic powers. When the God of Israel approaches, these powers must flee. The Canaanites will find themselves weak and vulnerable when the time for battle comes, but only the eye of faith can see this beforehand. This is the eye that looks to God and his promises instead of to outward conditions. Then it sees a way through the most difficult circumstances.

A Rebel and His Sons

Parashat Korach, Numbers 16:1–18:32

Moses endures a number of rebellions against his authority and responds each time with characteristic meekness. When the people build the Golden Calf, and later when they accept the negative report of the ten spies and refuse to enter the Promised Land, he even intercedes before God on their behalf. Likewise when Aaron and Miriam rebel against Moses, he does not speak a word in his own defense, and in the end prays for Miriam's restoration.

Why then, when the Levite Korach initiates a rebellion, does Moses call for divine judgment, and judgment of the harshest sort?

> By this you shall know that it is Adonai who sent me to do all these things and that they are not from my own heart: if these men die the death of all men, if the lot of all men comes upon them, it was not Adonai who sent me. But if Adonai creates a new thing, and the earth opens its mouth and swallows them and all that is theirs, and they go down alive into Sheol, then you shall know that these men have provoked Adonai. (Num. 16:28–30)

Note that Moses calls upon the Lord to "create" a punishment for Korach. The Hebrew verb is *bara*, which is used only with God as its subject. It implies not just a divine intervention through natural means, but a special creation out of nothing, a penalty that is clearly and undeniably of God. What is it about the rebellion of Korach and his supporters that elicits such a response?

We may understand Korach's rebellion more fully by comparing it with the challenge of Miriam and Aaron in Numbers 12. Moses' siblings attack their (younger) brother with the words,

"Has Adonai spoken only through Moses? Has he not spoken through us as well?" This statement is true, as far as it goes, but Adonai reminds Miriam and Aaron that Moses has received revelation on a much higher plane than they have. He is the Lord's unique spokesman and not to be challenged.

God silences Miriam and Aaron, but Korach carries their challenge further. He would put all Israel, not just Miriam and Aaron, on an equal footing with Moses: "It is too much for you! For the whole congregation, all of them, are holy, and Adonai is among them. Why do you exalt yourselves over the congregation of Adonai?" (16:3) Again, there is truth to the challenge. Korach is citing the Lord's promise to Israel at Mount Sinai: "You shall be to me a holy nation and a kingdom of priests" (Exod. 19:5). If all the people are holy, how can Moses and Aaron exalt themselves over them? But of course, they have not exalted themselves—Adonai has exalted them. Korach reaches a new level of rebellion by claiming that this divine election did not happen at all, and that Moses and Aaron are merely self-appointed leaders who are serving themselves.

If Korach's challenge were allowed to stand, it would undermine the authority not just of Moses and Aaron, but of the entire Torah received at Mount Sinai. After all, if Moses merely exalted himself, then his claim to speak for God is invalid, and his revelation is merely a human document. If the whole people is equally holy, and no one within it is unique, then it may produce many holy books on a par with Torah and many spiritual pathways from which to choose. Such a challenge merits the unique response that Moses invoked.

Since all the people are holy, Korach implies, there must be a strict egalitarianism among them that does not permit any to emerge as a leader. Or, if leaders do emerge, they must lead only by consensus and reflect the sentiments of the populace. Such ideas may be acceptable within human government, but they undermine the idea that there is a God who has authority over the affairs of men. Ultimately Korach challenges not only Moses and the Torah, but the sovereignty of God.

When he first hears Korach's challenge, Moses falls on his face, and then says, "In the morning the Lord will show who are His . . ." (16:5)

What is the reason why He chose such a time? R. Nathan explained: The Holy One, blessed be He, said: "If all the magicians of the world were to assemble and try to turn the morning into evening, they would not be able to do so, and as I made a partition between light and darkness, so have I set Aaron apart to sanctify him as most holy." (Num. Rabbah 18.4)

The Exodus from Egypt, the giving of Torah, and the establishment of the Aaronic priesthood, are not to be pre-empted by human ambitions and enterprises. The Lord orchestrates it all, and lifts up whom he will. When Moses calls upon him to "create a new thing" in response to Korach's rebellion, it is not only to stop Korach, but also to demonstrate that the whole plan belongs to God.

Korach, along with "all the people who were with [him] and all their possessions" (16:32) are swallowed up, as Moses said they would be. Torah tells us later (26:11), however, that the sons of Korach survived, because, as Ramban explains, "they were adults, righteous and good men, and their merit stood in their stead." Rashi indicates that the sons repented in the midst of the rebellion. When the earth opened its mouth to swallow their father's household, God provided a ledge of earth as a refuge for them and they survived.

The descendants of Korach, Levites like their ancestor, became worship leaders in Israel and several psalms are attributed to them. Psalm 42, the first of these psalms, reveals an entirely different attitude from that of the father. Korach challenged Moses and Aaron because he wanted to be exalted. The sages say that he was not satisfied to be a Levite but envied Aaron's role as Kohen Gadol and his proximity to the things of God. In contrast, the sons of Korach are content to be among the multitude that worships God. This attitude saves them from destruction and gives them a legacy as psalmists in Israel.

> As the deer pants for the water brooks,
> So pants my soul for You, O God.
> My soul thirsts for God, for the living God.
> When shall I come and appear before God . . .?
> For I used to go with the multitude;
> I went with them to the house of God,
> With the voice of joy and praise,
> With a multitude that kept a pilgrim feast. (Psa. 42:1–2, 4, NKJV).

The Serpent in the Wilderness

Parashat Hukkat, Numbers 19:1–22:1

The name of this parasha comes from the phrase in its second verse, "This is the decree of Torah—*hukkat haTorah* . . ." The specific decree it is referring to is the law of the red heifer, a law that commentators since the earliest times have considered mysterious and paradoxical.

Briefly, this decree states that an unblemished red heifer that has never been placed under the yoke is to be slaughtered outside the camp in the presence of the High Priest. It is burned in its entirety and its ashes are kept in a safe place to be mixed with the water of ritual purification. But, although the ashes of the red heifer make one ritually clean, the one who burned the cow, the one who handled the ashes, and even the High Priest who observed the process, are all rendered unclean thereby. The ashes of the red heifer are essential for the water of purification, but they render those that prepare them impure.

Rabbi Yochanan explained,

> It is not the corpse that causes contamination nor the water that purifies! The Holy One merely says, "I have laid down a statute; I have issued a decree. You are not allowed to transgress my decree," as it is written, *This is hukkat haTorah—the decree of the law.* (Numbers Rabbah 19:8)

The law of the red heifer is a חק (*hok*), a decree that makes little sense to the natural mind, but is given by God, so that we are not to question it. We may not understand a hok, but we are still to obey it as an act of faith, humbling the intellect in the presence of the Giver of Torah.

Shortly after receiving the paradoxical decree of the red heifer, the people will be given another one. They had again fallen into murmuring and complaining against God and Moses, and God responded dramatically.

And the LORD sent fiery serpents among the people, and they bit the people; and many people of Israel died. And the people came to Moses, and said: "We have sinned, because we have spoken against the LORD, and against you; pray to the LORD, that He take away the serpents from us." And Moses prayed for the people. And the LORD said to Moses: "Make a fiery serpent, and set it upon a pole; and it shall come to pass, that every one that is bitten, when he looks upon it, will live." And Moses made a serpent of copper, and set it upon the pole; and it came to pass, that if a serpent had bitten any man, when he looked to the serpent of copper, he lived. (21:6–9)

Surely, the copper serpent is a hok, a divine decree that is beyond human reason. The image of death becomes a source of life. A serpent brings death as punishment for sin, but the sinner who is bitten may look upon a serpent and live . . . unless he balks because the decree makes no sense. The one whose obedience overshadows his understanding will live.

Additionally, the word for pole is נֵס (*nes*), which normally means a sign or banner. God provides the image of judgment as a sign of his mercy. Those who heed the sign will live. A hok requires the response of obedience; a sign only requires a gaze. Yet both may require us to go beyond the limits of our own understanding.

The image itself had no power, of course. The sages said, "Does a serpent cause death or life? Rather, when they looked upward and subjected their hearts to their Father in Heaven they were healed, but if not, they died" (Rosh Hashanah 29a). The image cannot save; faith, repentance, and God's mercy alone spare the Israelites.

The image was preserved for centuries after the Exodus and named Nechushtan, based on both *nachash*—serpent—and *nechoshet*—copper. It possessed no power, but had become an object of worship, until it was finally destroyed in the reforms of Hezekiah.

He removed the high places, and broke the pillars, and cut down the Asherah; and he broke in pieces the copper serpent that Moses had made; for until those days the children of Israel brought offerings to it; and it was called Nechushtan. (2 Kings 18:4)

True, the image cannot save, but we may still wonder why God would use an image of the source of death to become the source of life. Rashi links this serpent to the serpent in the Garden, the original tempter. In the Garden, the serpent used malicious words to deny God's warning to Eve against eating of the tree of life. "Then the serpent said to the woman, 'You will not surely die. For God knows that in the day you eat of it your eyes will be opened, and you will be like God, knowing good and evil'" (Gen. 3:4–5).

The serpent not only lied, but it slandered God's motive in forbidding Eve and Adam to eat from the tree. In the end it was cursed by God. Therefore, in the incident in the wilderness, according to Rashi, God said, "Let the snake, who was stricken over bringing forth malicious talk, come and take his due from those who bring forth malicious talk."

The copper serpent represents not only the superficial source of suffering, but the underlying source—sin, unbelief, slander against God, and resistance to his purposes. Perhaps in looking toward it, each Israelite must acknowledge all this about himself.

Yeshua deepens the mystery of this *hukkat haTorah*: "And as Moses lifted up the serpent in the wilderness, even so must the Son of Man be lifted up, that whoever believes in Him should not perish but have eternal life" (John 3:14–15). Like the serpent, Yeshua will be lifted up . . . by crucifixion. Upon the Roman execution stake he will become a sign of death, judgment, and divine curse, "for he that is hanged is accursed of God" (Deut. 21:23). Yet, this sign becomes the source of life to those who look upon it in faith.

Here is a great mystery. This is not a sign that human reasoning would have devised. And indeed the human intellect has often found it repugnant. God again provides a sign of his mercy in the image of judgment. Blessed is the one whose obedience overshadows his understanding.

Balaam the Soothsayer

Parashat Balak, Numbers 22:2–25:9

One of the most profound and beautiful statements ever made about Israel—a statement recited to this day whenever a Jew enters the synagogue for the morning prayers—comes from the mouth of a gentile false prophet named Balaam. This Balaam had apparently gained genuine revelation from God, but he also accepted the offer of payment from the king of Moab in exchange for cursing Israel. Indeed, Balaam was so eager to earn the wages of cursing that he rose up in the morning and saddled his own donkey to go with the princes of Moab, who had come the day before to hire him (Num. 22:21).

The Talmud (Sanhedrin 105b) notes that it is beneath Balaam's dignity as a prophet to saddle his own donkey, but hatred for Israel and eagerness for payment motivate him. The Talmud contrasts Balaam with Abraham who also "disregards the rule of dignified conduct" to rise early and saddle his own donkey. But he does so out of love, in eagerness to obey God's command to offer up Isaac. Furthermore the Torah says *vayakam Bilam baboker*—"Balaam rose in the morning"—but *vayashkem Avraham baboker*—"Abraham rose **early** in the morning." Both love and hate disregard the rule of dignified conduct, but love proves more zealous. Abraham rises earlier than Balaam.

Balaam may be especially eager because Israel seems ripe for a curse. The Book of Numbers traces numerous complaints and rebellions, culminating in Israel's refusal to enter the Promised Land, and the penalty; that generation will die in the wilderness. Paradoxically, though, Israel begins to win battles; they defeat Sihon and Og, and apparently are being blessed by God. These victories strike fear in the heart of Israel's enemies, and particularly Balak, the King of Moab, who hires Balaam.

Balaam does not perceive the blessing upon Israel and sees only an enemy that is dangerous, but apparently vulnerable to the curse that, motivated by greed and hatred, he is ready to deliver. Here is the heart of the story: Balaam sees well enough with his eyes, but lacks spiritual vision. In the end he will gain spiritual vision, but still must make a choice that we also face: which shall we live by—natural vision or spiritual?

Balaam's blindness is apparent from the start. As he begins his journey, his donkey sees what he cannot:

> Then God's anger was aroused because he went, and the Angel of the Lord took his stand in the way as an adversary against him. And he was riding on his donkey, and his two servants were with him. Now **the donkey saw** the Angel of the Lord standing in the way with his drawn sword in his hand, and the donkey turned aside. . . . Then the Angel of the Lord stood in a narrow path between the vineyards, with a wall on this side and a wall on that side. And when **the donkey saw** the Angel of the Lord, she pushed herself against the wall. . . . Then the Angel of the Lord went further, and stood in a narrow place where there was no way to turn either to the right hand or to the left. And when **the donkey saw** the Angel of the Lord, she lay down under Balaam . . .
>
> Then the Lord opened Balaam's eyes, and **he saw** the Angel of the Lord standing in the way with his drawn sword in his hand; and he bowed his head and fell flat on his face. (22:22–27, 31, NKJV; emphasis mine)

Balaam is the seer, but his greed and hatred for Israel blind his eyes. The donkey's eyes are open all along and she sees the Angel of the Lord three times, but Balaam sees nothing until the Lord opens his eyes. When Balaam finally arrives at the edge of the encampment of Israel, his eyes remain open to see Israel's true condition in the sight of God:

> And Balaam **raised his eyes**, and **saw** Israel encamped according to their tribes; and the Spirit of God came upon him. Then he took up his oracle and said:

The utterance of Balaam the son of Be'or,
The utterance of the man whose **eyes are opened**,
The utterance of him who hears the words of God,
Who **sees** the vision of the Almighty,
Who falls down, with **eyes wide open** . . .
(24:2–4, NKJV; emphasis mine)

Ironically, when Balaam's eyes are opened he, the prophet-for-hire, can see Israel better than anyone else. At this low point in Israel's history, when they are still wandering in the wilderness because of sin, Balaam sees the ideal Israel and first utters the words that form the opening of the daily synagogue service: "How lovely are your tents, O Jacob! Your dwellings, O Israel!"

Now that his eyes are open Balaam sees four qualities that characterize God's people, despite appearances to the contrary, and despite the fact that they are undeserved.

Like valleys that stretch out,
Like gardens by the riverside,
Like aloes planted by the LORD,
Like cedars beside the waters.
He shall pour water from his buckets,
And his seed shall be in many waters. (24:6–7, NKJV)

Israel is like a garden; despite its apparent disunity and lack of direction, Israel possesses **order** and **fruitfulness**. Where the natural eye would see Israel *b'midbar*, in the barren wilderness, the enlightened eye sees a watered garden.

His king shall be higher than Agag,
And his kingdom shall be exalted. . .
Blessed is he who blesses you,
And cursed is he who curses you. (24:7, 9, NKJV)

Likewise, Israel in the wilderness is not a mere collection of tribes that have lost their way, but a kingdom possessing **power** and **divine protection**. Balaam comes to curse, but is given the vision to see that Israel is protected from the curse. Once he gains that vision he is unable to pronounce the curse at all. Still Balaam has a choice: will he live by his newly gained spiritual vision or by natural vision?

The Torah tells us that Balaam continued to seek Israel's downfall, and advised the Moabites to entice Israel to sin so that they would lose the blessing (31:16). In the end according to Joshua 13:22, "the children of Israel slay with the sword Balaam, the son of Be'or, the soothsayer." The Talmud (Sanhedrin 106a) discusses this statement: "A soothsayer! But he was a prophet!—Rabbi Yohanan said: At first he was a prophet, but subsequently he was a soothsayer."

A prophet stands in the counsels of the Almighty; a soothsayer is a mere fortune-teller, in violation of the prohibition of occult practices in Deuteronomy 18. Because Balaam misused his gift, he descended from prophecy to soothsaying. It is not spiritual knowledge that counts the most, but agreeing with the will of God; not vision but obedience that gains approval.

A Righteous Zealot

Parashat Pinchas, Numbers 25:10–30:1

Now HaShem spoke to Moses saying:
Pin'has . . . has turned my venomous-anger from the Children of Israel in his being-zealous with my jealousy in their midst, so that I did not finish off the Children of Israel in my jealousy.

Therefore say:
Here, I give him my covenant of *shalom*; and it shall be for him and for his seed after him a covenant of everlasting priesthood—because that he was zealous for his God, and effected-appeasement for the Children of Israel. (Num. 25:10–13; *The Schocken Bible*)

Religious zeal has become suspect in our day. We can easily list numerous current disputes, ranging from domestic to international, that originate in opposing religious ideologies. In Israel, we have seen religious zeal lead a young man to assassinate Prime Minister Rabin and claim that he was acting for God, or fuel conflicts between different Jewish parties over praying rights at the Western Wall. Yet, when Pinchas displays religious zeal, he receives the highest commendation. Moreover, his zeal seems to be of the most extreme type; he summarily executes Zimri a prince of the tribe of Shimon, and his Midianite consort, Kozbi, for violating God's Law.

Why does the Torah find the zeal of Pinchas so commendable? Is it not concerned that his example of taking justice into his own hands might be abused?

The early commentators seem to have had similar concerns about the possibility of misguided religious zeal. They insisted that

Pinchas was acting with the bounds of established authority. Thus the Talmud in Sanhedrin 82a says that Zimri brought Kozbi into the camp of Israel to challenge Moses, who himself had a Midianite wife, Zipporah. Rashi comments that Moses married Zipporah before the Torah was given. At the time of the giving of Torah, he continues, all Israel underwent a mass conversion, in which Zipporah was included so that she was no longer a heathen.

Nonetheless, Moses was so shaken by Zimri's challenge that he became speechless. Then, the Talmud continues, Pinchas "saw" (Num. 25:7) this challenge to Moses, and said, "O great-uncle, did you not teach us on your descent from Mount Sinai that he who cohabits with a heathen woman is to be punished by zealots?" Moses replied, "He who reads the letter, let him be the agent to carry it out." Thus, Pinchas was given the authority to act as he did.

The earliest commentary on this incident appears in Psalm 106 (vss. 28–31). The psalm views the matter more simply, as the visceral response of a righteous man confronted by idolatry:

> And they clung to Ba'al Peor and ate the sacrifices of the
> dead.
> They angered him with their behavior and a plague broke
> out among them.
> Pinchas arose and executed judgment and the plague was
> halted.
> It was accounted to him as a righteous deed for all genera-
> tions, forever.

Whether authorized or not, Pinchas' act of rising up to execute judgment was accounted to him as righteousness forever. The circumstances of his story help us distinguish between a commendable zeal for God and the misguided religious zeal that disgraces God's name.

Pinchas is introduced as "the son of Eleazar the son of Aaron the priest" (25:7). He is of the line of the Kohen Gadol, charged with handling and protecting the holy things in Israel. When Zimri defied the authority of Moses and the priesthood, and thereby of God, all the people stood at the door of the tent of meeting and wept. It was up to the priest to arise and defend the Torah.

A similar issue arose in the career of Messiah, when he took it upon himself to drive the moneychangers out of the Temple courts.

When his disciples saw Yeshua acting this way, they remembered the words of Psalm 69:10, "Zeal for your house has consumed me" (John 2:17). The root word in both the psalm and in our parasha is קָנָא (*kana*), meaning to be envious, jealous, or zealous. It is a word Adonai employs in the Second Commandment to describe himself: "You shall have no other gods before me. You shall not make for yourself a graven image . . . you shall not bow down to them or worship them, for I Adonai your God am אֵל קַנָּא (*El Kana*; The Jealous God)" (Exod. 20:3–5).

Idolatry is the key to our story. The jealousy or zeal of God arises in the face of idolatry. Zimri's offense is not only sexual immorality, but also the worship of idols that accompanied it. Israel went after not just the Midianite women, but the Ba'al of Peor. Likewise, the moneychangers' offense was not merely greed. Rather, by making the Temple of the Lord a place of merchandising, they were worshiping the false god Mammon.

The priest is responsible to combat idolatry, to be jealous on behalf of the jealous God. Pinchas is rewarded with an eternal priesthood because he has shown himself to be a priest indeed. Yet when Yeshua acted to purify the Temple courts, it was not so clear who he was, and therefore, whether he had authority to act. So his opponents challenged him, "What sign do you show us, seeing that you do these things?" (John 2:18) In other words, they wanted him to prove that he had the authority to act upon his zeal. Yeshua cryptically referred to his future resurrection: "Destroy this temple and in three days I will raise it up again" (2:19). This would be the sign of his authority to combat the idolatry that had infected the Temple courts, and that would eventually bring judgment upon them.

Schocken Bible translator Everett Fox writes, "For the biblical writers, idolatry was the worst of all crimes." Idolatry demands judgment. God's response to the idolatry of Ba'al Peor is to send a plague among the Israelites. Before Pinchas acted, the Lord had instructed Moses to execute the chief perpetrators, "so that the fierce anger of the Lord may turn away from Israel" (Num. 25:4). When Pinchas arose to stop the plague, 24,000 idolaters had already perished. His act of zeal "made atonement for the children of Israel" (25:13). Significantly, Yeshua also makes atonement for Israel. The sign of his Messiahship is the resurrection, an event that is ultimately redemptive.

Religious zeal often seems like a plague in today's world, yet Pinchas' zeal averts a plague. He displays the distinguishing mark of righteous zeal. It rises up, not in defense of a religious party, nor of holy sites, nor of ethnic or political dominance, but only to counter idolatry. Its purpose is never victory or revenge, but is always redemptive, bringing atonement for those who have offended El Kana, the Jealous God, and restoring them to him.

The Bond of Community

Parashat Mattot, Numbers 30:2–32:42

What holds a nation together? The Torah is—among many other things—a book about nationhood and how it works. The formation of Adat Yisrael, the congregation of Israel, and the rules and customs that are to govern it, has implications for Israel as a nation today, and for other nations, organizations, communities, and even families, as well.

The tribes of Reuben and Gad come to Moses with a request for land on the east side of the Jordan, land outside the boundaries promised to the children of Israel (32:1–5). Reuben and Gad appear to be motivated by the bottom line: "They saw the land of Jazer and the land of Gilead and behold, it was a place for livestock." The land is rich and abundant. Here the two tribes can pursue their livelihood with a great prospect for success.

Reuben and Gad were thinking of community as primarily a setting for success and prosperity. Such a vision seems to be triumphant in our day, as political ideologies disintegrate under the pressures of the global market place. In Israel, the old Zionist ideals seem to have given way to the urge to join the ranks of stable, capitalist democracies. Moses reminds the two tribes, and us, that true community—and true nationhood—is founded on something more profound. God has commanded Israel to take possession of the land beyond the Jordan. The community of Israel is held together by more than a shared desire for the good life; rather, it shares in an assignment from God.

The Promised Land is more than a nice place to raise a family. Rather, it is the inheritance of Israel forever, a place from which God will display his goodness and authority to all nations. There may have been other lands readily available for settlement that would have met Israel's physical needs. But the story of the Exodus from Egypt must end not just in national liberation, but in Eretz Yisrael, the place of divine destiny.

This shared destiny implies a shared assignment. Only if the two tribes will join in the conquest of the Promised Land will they be given land east of the Jordan. The tribes announce that this was their intention all along; they say that they "will build enclosures for our livestock, and cities for our children" (32:16) and then join the rest of Israel in conquering the Promised Land. Rashi comments,

> They were more concerned for their property than for their sons and daughters, for they mention their livestock before their children. Moses said to them, "This is not right! Put the first things first, and the secondary second. First build cities for your children and then make pens for your livestock."

Greed gets in the way of the greater vision that holds community together. When we reduce community to a venue for material advancement, we lose it altogether. If we shrink from the shared assignment, we lose the shared destiny.

In the midst of these negotiations, a third party joins Reuben and Gad, the half-tribe of Manasseh (32:33). Their sudden appearance in the story is a bit puzzling and various explanations have been proposed. Perhaps the most likely explanation is that Manasseh's involvement serves to bind Reuben and Gad to the rest of Israel. Torah places a great emphasis on the wholeness and integrity of each tribe. If one tribe settles partly west of the Jordan and partly to the east, it binds together the two sides of the river into one community. It provides a conduit for the greater holiness of Eretz Yisrael to influence the land to the east.

Later Moses will introduce an ordinance that also serves to bind together the community (35:9–34). Once the tribes enter the Land of Canaan they are to designate cities of refuge, where a manslayer can flee from the relatives of his victim, who are entitled to kill him in revenge. The Torah does not ban the ancient custom that gives a close relative the right to avenge the death of a family member, but it regulates its practice. This custom is an aspect of the responsibilities of the *go'el*, the kinsman-redeemer, that play such a key role in the story of Ruth. Here, however, the go'el does not rescue a relative from poverty but avenges his death.

The city of refuge provides a sanctuary for the manslayer until the court determines whether he acted intentionally or not. If the killing was accidental, he may remain in the city of refuge until the death of the High Priest, at which time he is free from bloodguilt and may return home. If the court rules that he acted intentionally, that he is indeed a murderer, he is cast out of the city of refuge and the go'el may kill him when he encounters him.

Surprisingly, Torah ordains that there are to be three cities of refuge in Eretz Yisrael (the land of Israel) and three on the east bank of the Jordan. Only two and a half tribes live on the east bank, and the population is much smaller, but it shares equally in the system of the cities of refuge. Furthermore, the ordinance of the city of refuge concludes with words that would seem to apply only to Eretz Yisrael proper, yet the ruling is in effect on both sides of the Jordan (35:33–34):

> You shall not bring guilt upon the land in which you are, for the blood will bring guilt upon the Land; the Land will not have atonement for the blood that was spilled in it, except through the blood of the one who spilled it. You shall not contaminate the Land that you inhabit, in whose midst I dwell, for I am Adonai who dwells among the Children of Israel.

There are equal numbers of cities on both sides of the Jordan to affirm the unity of the Children of Israel. Despite different dwellings and priorities, all Israel is encompassed within the same Torah. Today this truth may continue to bind together the Jews of Israel and the Jews of the Diaspora. Adonai makes it clear that he dwells not only in the midst of Eretz Yisrael, but also among the Children of Israel wherever they dwell. He still has an assignment for the whole nation of Israel.

Community is a task, a calling, and not a passive agreement. A community stays together not just by allowing every member to seek "life, liberty, and the pursuit of happiness," but by working toward the same vision. In our day of pluralism we see how difficult this shared vision can be, and how elusive true community has become. Like so much that originates in God, it is difficult to translate into secular terms. When divine revelation is the source of community, the divine assignment holds it together.

Guard Your Inheritance

Parashat Masa'ei, Numbers 33:1–35:13

The Book of Numbers concludes with the division of the Promised Land among the twelve tribes, even before the tribes have crossed the Jordan to take possession of it. Throughout Numbers, Israel has rebelled and resisted God's purpose. Earlier in the book, they refused to enter the Promised Land, and so were sentenced to forty years of wandering. Discord and rebellion often marked these years, but now the account will end on a note of hope.

In the process of division, a difficult question arises. The daughters of Zelophehad, a man of the tribe of Manasseh, come before Moses and the leaders of Israel. As women, they have no direct share in the inheritance of the land. Normally, they would partake of this blessing as part of a household led by a male, their father, brother, or husband. But Zelophehad has died leaving no sons. His daughters are concerned that his name and inheritance will be lost from among his family, and they request, "Give us a possession among our father's brothers" (27:4).

Moses consults with the Lord, who upholds the daughters' claim, and uses their precedent to establish a law.

> And you shall speak to the children of Israel, saying: "If a man dies and has no son, then you shall cause his inheritance to pass to his daughter. If he has no daughter, then you shall give his inheritance to his brothers. If he has no brothers, then you shall give his inheritance to his father's brothers. And if his father has no brothers, then you shall give his inheritance to the relative closest him in his family, and he shall possess it." And it shall be to the children of Israel a statute of judgment, just as the LORD commanded Moses. (27:8–10, NKJV)

We find ourselves rooting for the daughters and delighted that they are vindicated. We admire their chutzpah as they approach Moses directly and call for a radical new ruling. This is, after all, a patriarchal society where women rarely speak. Later, however, as recounted in this week's parasha, the male relatives of Zelophehad bring an objection, and we fear that the story will revert to business as usual.

If the daughters acquire Zelophehad's property, his kinsmen say, then if they marry men from other tribes, the property will pass out of the inheritance of the tribe of Manasseh altogether. The sons of such a union would be heirs of the property of Zelophehad, and they would be members of the tribe of their father, not of their mother. The property would revert to their tribal allotment.

After hearing this objection, Moses again consults with the Lord, and then decrees that the daughters of Zelophehad may "marry whom they think best, but they may marry only within the family of their father's tribe" (36:6). Thus their inheritance will remain part of the holding of Manasseh.

At first glance, this story reveals some of the classic tensions between men and women. The women seem to be motivated by love for their father and the honor of his name. They are concerned with family and with maintaining its wholeness. The men focus on property, and on protecting the integrity of the tribe's land holdings. The initial enactment in favor of the daughters of Zelophehad is revolutionary, in this instance at least placing the women on an equal footing with the men. After the men appeal, however, the women's status is limited again. They are given a share of the inheritance, but their freedom to marry is curtailed for the sake of tribal continuity.

Beneath these surface tensions, however, there is a remarkable unity, which may serve as a model of male-female relationships in our own day. Both the daughters of Zelophehad and his kinsmen are concerned with both family and property. The two cannot be viewed separately: Family wholeness is preserved as the family inheritance is kept intact.

When the daughters of Zelophehad were introduced in Chapter 27, the Torah said, "Then came the daughters of Zelophehad, the son of Hepher, the son of Gilead, the son of Machir, the son of Manasseh, of the families of Manasseh the son of Joseph. . ." Rashi comments that this last phrase stresses the daughters' relationship to Joseph,

Why is this stated? Has it not already said "Son of Manasseh"? But it is stated to tell you that Joseph held the land precious, as it says, "And you shall bring up my bones [to the land of Israel." Gen. 50:25], and his daughters held the land precious, as it says, "Give us a possession." And it is stated to teach you that they were all righteous . . .

The daughters are not motivated by greed, but for love of the land. The inheritance of land is not a strictly material possession. Rather, it represents the family's share in the legacy of Israel, its stake in the community and heritage of the chosen people. Such a share is essential to the more "feminine," relational aspects of family. A healthy family cannot exist in isolation, but must be part of community.

Likewise, we should not view the kinsmen of Zelophehad as motivated by mere greed. Apparently, there is a higher principle involved, because the Lord endorses their position. Like the daughters, they are concerned with preserving the family heritage. The daughters are thinking of the portion of their father; the kinsmen are thinking of the larger portion of the tribe. Both the men and the women, however, share a vision of the value and inviolability of the divine inheritance.

The shared principle is this: "The inheritance of the Children of Israel is not to go round from tribe to tribe; indeed, each-one to the inheritance of his father's tribe is to cleave, (among) the Children of Israel" (36:7; *The Schocken Bible*). As each family preserves its heritage, it is strengthened, and the larger good is advanced as well.

The story ends on a happy note. The daughters of Zelophehad comply with the ruling and marry "whom they think best" among the sons of their own tribe. The Torah finds a way to reconcile the legitimate desires of the individual and the community's need for stability, a reconciliation that has eluded us in the modern world. The Book of Numbers, which recounts so much rebellion against God, ends with an account of faithful submission.

The message for us today is that it requires both the feminine and the masculine perspective to keep the community whole. The daughters of Zelophehad teach us to take hold of our inheritance in a way that strengthens our community.

דברים
The Book of Deuteronomy

Deuteronomy, the final book of Torah, differs from the rest of the books in a number of ways. Its Hebrew name is D'varim or words, from the opening line, "These are the words which Moses spoke to all Israel on this side of the Jordan in the wilderness, in the plain opposite Suph . . ." Deuteronomy comprises Moses' retelling of the entire Exodus story to a new generation, the Children of Israel about to enter the land of promise.

The whole book takes place in the plains of Moab and concludes with a brief narrative portion recounting the anointing of Joshua as the new leader, and the death of Moses. Only in the final verses does the scene shift from the plains of Moab to nearby Mount Nebo, where Moses gazes upon the Promised Land before he dies.

> And since then there has not arisen in Israel a prophet like Moses, whom the LORD knew face to face, in all the signs and wonders which the LORD sent him to do in the land of Egypt, before Pharaoh, before all his servants, and in all his land, and by all that mighty power and all the great terror which Moses performed in the sight of all Israel. (34:10–12, NKJV)

As a retelling of Torah, Deuteronomy reiterates all the major themes of the first four books, but it also adds an emphasis of its own. It is an extended sermon in which Moses reminds an entire generation of their divine destiny, and he speaks with an authority that brings his sermon to life for all future generations. Deuteronomy embodies the sense of Torah as instruction; it is the inspired instruction in how to know and serve the God who has delivered Israel from bondage and brought them into their inheritance.

The form of Deuteronomy reflects the covenant treaty documents of the ancient Near East, which defined and protected the relationship between a mighty king and his vassals. In Deuteronomy, God is the mighty king, who has made a covenant with Abraham and his descendants that he will be their God and they will be his people.

This relationship is expressed in covenant love, which is a dominant theme throughout Deuteronomy.

It is significant that Deuteronomy contains the great expression of covenant love between God and Israel known as the Shema, which has shaped the Jewish consciousness in every generation.

> Hearken O Israel:
> HaShem our God, HaShem is One!
> Now you are to love HaShem your God
> with all your heart, with all your being, with all your substance!
> (6:4–5; *The Schocken Bible*)

Time to Move On

Parashat D'varim, Deuteronomy 1:1–3:22

Adonai our God spoke to us at Horev, saying:
Enough for you, staying at this mountain!
(1:6, *Schocken Bible*)

Deuteronomy is entitled *D'varim* in Hebrew, from its opening phrase, "These are the words (*d'varim*) that Moses spoke to all Israel." This last of the books of Torah comprises a series of speeches that Moses gives to a new generation of Israelites, those who are about to enter the Promised Land. Moses begins with a review of the travels of Israel from Sinai to the east bank of the Jordan, which is the setting for the entire book.

The words that God uses to send Israel off from Sinai, or Horev, are striking: "Enough for you—*rav lachem*—of staying at this mountain!" Sinai is the holy mountain, the place of divine encounter and the giving of Torah, yet this command seems rather abrupt, almost a rebuke. The tone continues in the verse following: "Face about, march on and come to the Amorite hill country. . ."

In the plain sense, the phrase may simply indicate that the year that Israel has encamped at Sinai is long enough; it is time to continue on to the land of Canaan. Rashi, however, brings out a further meaning, based on a midrash that understands *rav lachem* as meaning "there is much for you":

> There is much eminence for you, and reward for your having dwelt at this mountain. You made the tabernacle, menorah, and holy implements, you received the Torah, and you appointed Sanhedrin courts for yourselves, of leaders of thousands and leaders of hundreds.

This reading is undoubtedly true. Sinai is the place of great reward, the place of an encounter with God that elevated Israel to greatness. Yet this reading does not exhaust the implications of the phrase *rav lachem*. These same words were part of the debate between Moses and the supporters of Korach during the great rebellion of Numbers 16.

> They assembled against Moses and against Aaron and said
>   to them:
> *Rav lachem*—Too much is yours!
> Indeed, the entire community, the entirety-of-them, are
>   holy, and in their midst is Adonai!
> Why then do you exalt yourselves over the assembly of
>   Adonai? (vs. 3)

Moses answers this challenge with a challenge of his own, that they all appear before Adonai with their incense burners in their hands and let Adonai himself indicate whom he chooses as holy over his assembly. He concludes his challenge with the same phrase, "*Rav lachem*—Too much is yours, Sons of Levi!" (vs. 7)

In this setting the words are a rebuke. Could the phrase have the same sense in the command to depart Horev? And if so, for what would the Lord be rebuking Israel? He is certainly not minimizing the experience at Sinai, telling the people to move on from the Torah and all that it contains. Sinai is the place of an unparalleled divine encounter, the place of a revelation from God that has defined Israel's character and history ever since. Much of Deuteronomy reminds Israel **not** to depart from Sinai, in the sense of not departing from the original revelation and all its statutes, commandments, and ordinances. At the same time, the Lord seems to be warning Israel not to settle in on a particular experience with God, but to continue in obedience to fulfill God's purpose.

A sense of God's immediate presence is an unparalleled reward, but there is always the temptation in the spiritual journey to "camp out" at the place of our greatest experience of God. The experience itself can become the center of focus, and when it is gone, we seek a repeat performance. For some, the spiritual life becomes a desperate search for some old feeling of the divine, or for a new revelation to match the original one that initiated the journey.

Such a temptation may be especially acute for those who have had a life changing encounter with Yeshua as the living Messiah. Sha'ul on his way to Damascus to persecute the believers there had a life changing encounter with the divine. Overwhelmed by this encounter, Sha'ul asked two questions: first, "Who are you, Lord?" As at Sinai, this encounter was a revelation of God, and Sha'ul sought to understand the nature of this revelation. When he realized that the one who was speaking to him from heaven was Yeshua, Sha'ul, as a good Pharisee, asked the second question: "Lord, what do you want me to do?" The lesson of Sinai is that divine revelation is not the end of the journey, but the beginning of a new journey. The Lord said to Sha'ul, "Arise and go into the city, and you will be told what you must do" (Acts 9:5-6). "*Rav lachem*— Enough for you this supernatural encounter; now you must move on to the assignment for which I have called you."

Sha'ul's initial encounter contained the seed of his life-long ministry, for it was here that he encountered Yeshua as the living Messiah, the Lord of all. It was this vision of Yeshua that informed Sha'ul's lofty descriptions of Messiah in his letters and fueled his mission to the gentiles. If Yeshua is the Lord revealed from heaven, he is Lord of all humankind, gentiles as well as Jews. Yeshua's commission to Sha'ul to go to the gentiles flowed out of his self-revelation on the road to Damascus.

When the Lord sent Israel on from Horev, the high point of their journey from Egypt, he was teaching us to ask the two questions at our spiritual high points: "Lord who are you?" and "What do you want me to do?" We are not to camp out at our experience or to spend the rest our lives trying to recover it. After he commanded Israel to depart from Horev, the Lord said, "See, I give before you the land, enter, take-possession of the land . . ." (Deut. 1:8)

The spiritual journey does not consist of a few dramatic encounters with God between long detours through the wilderness. Rather it is a journey launched by the divine encounter, and perhaps fueled by further encounters, but directed toward the God-given assignment that defines our lives.

The Glories of Exile

Parashat Va'et'chanan, Deuteronomy 3:23–7:11

Va'et'chanan: *Now I pleaded with HaShem at that
time, saying. . .
Pray let me cross over
that I may see the good land
that is in the country across the Jordan,
this good hill-country, and the Lebanon!*
(Deut. 3:23, 25 *Schocken Bible*)

The Jewish soul was formed in exile. God first called Abraham outside the Land of Canaan. There also Jacob found his wives Leah
and Rachel, and his destiny as Israel, father of the twelve tribes. In
Egyptian exile, the nation of Israel became mighty and numerous.
In the wanderings of exile the nation first heard God's calling to be
a kingdom of priests and a holy nation. And, we may add, it was in
exile that this calling took the form by which we recognize it today.

Now in Parashat Va'et'chanan, Moses recounts the time when
God told him that he would die in exile. It is fitting that Tisha
B'Av often falls during the reading of this parasha, for it is the day
on which we remember the beginning of Israel's long exile in 586
BCE, when the temple of Jerusalem was destroyed by the
Chaldeans. On this same day six hundred and fifty years later the
Romans destroyed the rebuilt temple again.

Tisha b'Av mourns for the temple and the endless years of exile, but our parasha reminds us that exile is the domain of greatness
as well as sorrow. Moses our teacher lived his entire life in exile, and
achieved the highest degree of greatness, as did many of his followers in later centuries.

An ancient rabbinical story reflects a similar optimism concerning exile. A Jewish farmer is plowing his field when his ox lows. A

passing Arab says, "Israelite, Israelite, untie your ox, untie your plow, and take off your plowshare, for the Temple has been destroyed!" The farmer does as his Arab neighbor suggests, and then his ox lows a second time. The neighbor then proclaims, "Tie your ox, tie your plow, and put your plowshare back on, for the Messiah has been born!"

Despite the loss of the Temple, and the exile that follows, there is always hope for Israel. The Scriptures promise a final restoration ushered in by Messiah's return. The story implies the converse as well. The farmer possessed the land, but experienced the loss of the temple. The hope remains, but unbroken possession of the Promised Land was not yet guaranteed.

Today, the exile is over for any Jew who can find his way back to the Promised Land. The election of Ehud Barak in 1999 was generally seen as reflecting a desire for normalization and stability. With Jewish presence in the land assured, some Israelis suggest that Israel is just another nation among the nations, whose highest ambition is to have normal relations with its neighbors. Nevertheless, in the midst of such stability, the Jewish people still remembers Tisha b'Av. Even in the days of Zionist fulfillment we continue to mourn the loss of our sovereignty. The Jewish soul is as deeply formed by exile as by the Promised Land.

The story of the Jewish plowman was once cited in a medieval disputation, a Jewish-Catholic debate arranged by the Church to prove the truth of Roman Catholicism in the face of Jewish intransigence. Many such disputations were held, but the most famous took place in Barcelona and pitted a Jewish convert named Pablo Christiani against the great Torah commentator Ramban.

Pablo cited this story to prove that even the rabbinic sources recognized that the Messiah had already come, and therefore, according to his reasoning, must be the Jesus whom the Church venerated. Pablo, of course, was being naïve to invoke the Talmud to establish religious dogma. Ramban explained that the story was not meant as a literal chronology but, he claimed, even if the Messiah was born at that time, this does not mean that he has "come."

> Moses our teacher did not come on the day he was born, nor was he a redeemer at that time. However, when he came before Pharaoh by command of the Holy One,

blessed be He, and said to him, "Thus saith the Lord, the God of Israel: Let my people go," then he had come. Similarly, when the Messiah will come to the Pope and say to him by the command of God, "Let my people go," then he has come. To this day, however, he has not yet come.

Such *chutzpah* (nerve) did not serve Ramban well. The church authorities declared Pablo the winner of the disputation, and Ramban had to flee Spain for his safety. Ironically, his exile was a portent of the exile of the entire Jewish community of Spain 200 years later—on Tisha b'Av.

It may be that the lines are not so clear as Ramban imagined them. Regathered Israelis still mourn the exile and are not ready to consider themselves as living in the messianic age. Conversely, it may not have been so odd to imagine, as did Pablo, that the Messiah was present while Israel remained in exile.

In our parasha, when Moses pleads to be allowed to enter the Promised Land, the Lord responds, "*Rav-lach*; Enough for you! Do not speak to me again about this matter!" (Deut. 3:26) In the plain sense, the Lord is telling Moses that he has argued enough and needs to accept the divine decree; he will never enter the land. Rashi reads *Rav-lach* differently, as "It is much for you," implying "that more than this is in store for you; the great goodness which is hidden away for you." God reassures Moses that there will be reward enough for him in the age to come even without entering the Land in this age.

We might add this interpretation: *Rav-lach*; Enough for you! It is **much** for you, Moses, that you have the privilege of leading the chosen people out of bondage to meet with God on Mount Sinai and receive the Torah from his hand. All these events took place in exile, but they are enough and more than enough; it is much for you, even if you never enter the land of promise.

Circumcision of the Heart

Parashat Ekev, Deuteronomy 7:12–11:25

D'varim, the last of the five books of Moses, is the Torah's book of transformation. It envisions a new nature for the generation of Israelites who will enter the land. One of the clearest references to this transformation comes after Moses reminds the children of Israel of the events at Mount Sinai, including the golden calf. Even after this grievous sin, Adonai will forgive Israel and give them the Promised Land. Moses reminds them,

> Now, O Israel, what does Adonai your God require of you? Only to fear Adonai your God, to walk in all his ways and to love him, and to serve Adonai your God with all your heart and with all your soul, to observe the commandments of Adonai and his decrees which I command you today for your good. . . . Therefore circumcise the foreskins of your heart and stiffen your neck no longer. (10:12–16)

Israel is to respond to the mercy of Adonai by loving him wholeheartedly. This concept of love for God appears explicitly only once or twice in all the preceding books of Torah, but dominates the chapters of D'varim. After Moses reiterates the Ten Commandments, for example, he goes on to give what Messiah himself, and many of our other teachers, describe as the greatest commandment: "You shall love Adonai your God with all your heart, with all your soul, and with all your might" (6:5).

Likewise, in the passage above, Moses speaks of love for God, a response that is simple and ultimately fair. We are to love him wholeheartedly because he has first shown his love toward us. But something within our human nature blocks this love for God, and must be removed if we are to respond fully. Love for God requires a profound inward change, an inner transformation that Torah describes as the circumcision of the heart.

Circumcision is, of course, a highly significant term. In the simplest sense it is the removal of a covering or obstacle. Thus the *Stone Chumash* translates verse 16, "You shall cut away the barrier of your heart . . ." To genuinely love the Lord, which is the goal of D'varim, Israel must cut away the sin and unbelief that dull their hearts. Circumcision of the heart is a metaphor for repentance, return to the Lord. But there is more.

Circumcision of an infant boy on the eighth day is called *b'rit milah*, the covenant of circumcision. This ritual involves far more than the mere medical procedure to remove a fleshly covering. In the same way, the inward circumcision of which Moses speaks is more than just removal of the barrier of the heart. Circumcision of the heart is part of the covenant renewal that dominates the entire book of D'varim. As a new generation prepares to enter the Promised Land, it requires a renewed covenant to fulfill the agreement Adonai made with Israel at Sinai. Outward circumcision is the seal of the covenant; inward circumcision is the seal of renewed covenant.

Furthermore, circumcision implies a dedication of the eight-day-old infant to Adonai. At the conclusion of the ceremony we say, "Amen! Just as he has entered into the covenant, so may he enter into Torah, into the chuppah, and into good deeds!" In other words, circumcision seals the covenant once for all, but the covenant continues to define and direct the child for the rest of his life. He has been dedicated to Adonai. Likewise, the inward circumcision implies a life-long dedication of the Israelites to their God.

This three-fold meaning of circumcision of the heart—return to Adonai, renewed covenant, and life-long dedication—summarizes the transformation that is the goal of the book of D'varim. The phrase appears here as a command: "Therefore circumcise the foreskins of your heart. . ." Toward the end of the book the phrase appears again as a promise. Moses describes the future exile of Israel and its final ingathering to the Promised Land. Adonai will have mercy on his people and restore them to himself, even after their sin and wandering:

Then Adonai your God will bring you to the land that your fathers possessed and you will possess it. He will prosper you and multiply you more than your fathers. And Adonai your God will circumcise your heart and the heart of your seed to love Adonai your God with all your heart and with all your soul, that you may live. (Deut. 30:5–6)

D'varim teaches that, even after the deliverance from Egypt and the giving of Torah, restoration to Adonai requires a profound transformation that only God can provide. It is beyond human ability, but God promises to accomplish it for us. When is this promise of a circumcised heart to be fulfilled? Paul refers to it in Romans 2:28–29.

For he is not a Jew who is one outwardly, nor is circumcision that which is outward in the flesh; but he is a Jew who is one inwardly, and circumcision is that of the heart, in the spirit, not in the letter, whose praise is not from men but from God. (NKJV)

This passage is frequently misunderstood. Paul does not envision a new "spiritual" Israel to replace the old "fleshly" Israel. Rather, he repeats the promise of Torah that in the latter days Adonai himself will circumcise the heart of Israel. This is the goal of Torah and of God's redemptive work. In the end all Israel will be restored to Adonai and given a heart to love and serve him fully. Even now the Messiah has come to bring this transformation to those who accept him.

The Jewish people, says Paul, cannot boast simply because we possess Torah. Rather our praise comes from fulfilling Torah, a fulfillment that is only possible with the transformed heart that the spirit of God provides. It is the circumcised heart that is able to "love Adonai your God with all your heart and with all your soul, that you may live." And it is God himself who is able to circumcise the human heart.

A Word Ancient and New

Parashat Re'eh, Deuteronomy 11:26–16:17

Everything that I command you,
that *you are to take-care to observe,*
you are not to add to it, you are not to diminish from it!
(Deut. 13:1, *Schocken Bible*)

In its final book, Deuteronomy, Torah begins to see itself as "a final, closed, 'canonical' dispensation," in the words of *Schocken Bible* translator Everett Fox. Torah is given by the mouth of God and is distinct from every purely human document. Therefore human authors must not add to it or take from it. Already in an earlier parasha, Moses had commanded Israel:

You are not to add to the word that I am commanding you,
and you are not to subtract from it,
in keeping the commandments of HaShem your God that I
    am commanding you. (4:2)

Yeshua also spoke of the inalterability of Torah: "Do not think that I came to destroy the Torah or the Prophets. I did not come to destroy, but to fulfill. For assuredly I say to you, until heaven and earth pass away not the smallest letter or stroke will pass from the Torah until all is fulfilled" (Matt. 5:17–18). If Torah is given by the mouth of God, it must remain free from human embellishment or modification for all time.

This lofty view of Torah raises a question. How is the unchangeable body of Scripture to address all of the changing circumstances of life? Many aspects of contemporary life were simply unimaginable in the days of Moses. Thus, Torah instructs us not to murder, but permits capital punishment, warfare, and self-defense. How does this complex of laws apply to abortion and euthanasia, to our modern judicial system, to political assassination? Torah forbids labor on Shabbat; how does this ban apply to the use of modern "labor-saving" technologies on the holy day?

Long before the modern age, the sages seemed at times to add to Torah. For example, in discussing Deuteronomy 4:2, Ramban points out a difficulty with the rabbinical requirement of reading the megillah—the scroll of Esther—on Purim.

> The rabbis said, "It is written, 'These are the commandments that the LORD commanded Moses.' These are the commandments that we were ordered by the mouth of Moses, and Moses told us that no other prophet is destined to establish anything new for you—yet Mordecai and Esther want to establish something new for us!" The rabbis did not move from there while discussing the matter until the Holy One, blessed be He, enlightened their eyes.

When the Holy One enlightened their eyes, the rabbis were able to find the command to read the megillah implied in the Torah, Prophets, and Writings. Thus, they were not adding to Torah, but simply bringing to the fore something already written within it. Since the Torah contains all things, the rabbis taught, deep study of Torah would reveal truths that may not be evident to a more superficial reading. Thus, the unchanging word meets the needs of changing times.

This understanding of Torah answers another question that arises as we continue in Deuteronomy 13. Moses warns Israel against the danger of false prophets who would tell the people to serve strange new gods. Even if such a prophet gives a sign or wonder that comes to pass, the people are not to listen to him, but to serve only the LORD who brought them out of Egypt. This entire chapter is taken up with cautions about false prophecy, so that we might wonder why it does not ban prophecy altogether. Yet Deuteronomy not only regulates the use of prophecy, but declares in 18:15, "The LORD your God will raise up for you a prophet like me [Moses] from your midst, from your brethren. Him you shall hear."

If the Torah is complete and one may not add to nor subtract from it, what need is there for further prophecy? Apparently we need prophecy because so much that is within Torah is implicit. It is canon, a complete and perfect text that neither needs nor will tolerate any alternation. Yet this closed book is filled with meaning still to be discovered. The prophet does not bring a completely new word, but a word of Torah that has not yet been recognized. Here is a key to our use of Scripture today; we can be confident that it contains all that is needful to guide us, but we also know that it will take effort to discover its riches. We need not seek an entirely new word for the modern age; we need to dig more deeply into the ancient word.

When the rabbis of old agonized over the legitimacy of the requirement to read the megillah, the Lord enlightened their eyes to see it authorized within Torah. The prophet is one whose eyes are enlightened to recognize new truth in the Torah. Just as the Torah is given by God, so is this enlightenment. The prophet who speaks from his own inspiration or creativity is false: "'Behold, I am against the prophets,' declares the LORD, 'who use their tongues and declare, "The LORD declares". . . yet I did not send them or command them'" (Jer. 23:31–32).

Even Messiah himself, like the prophets, must speak and act in accord with Torah. After Yeshua rose from the dead, he appeared to his followers and told them,

> "These are the words I spoke to you while I was still with you, that all things which are written about me in the Torah of Moses and the prophets and the psalms must be fulfilled." Then he opened their minds to understand the Scriptures. He said to them, "Thus it is written, that the Messiah would suffer and rise again from the dead the third day, and that repentance for forgiveness of sins would be proclaimed in his name to all the nations, beginning from Jerusalem." (Luke 24:44–45)

Like the rabbis, the followers of Messiah cannot see what is implicit in Torah until their eyes are opened. He who gives the Torah also gives the enlightenment to see all that Torah contains.

A true prophet does not bring a completely new message, but opens the minds of his hearers to perceive the message given of old. The false prophet, Moses warned, would entice the people to follow gods that they had not known (Deut. 13:1). He would draw the people away from the God who brought them out of Egypt, to worship gods whom neither they nor their fathers had known (13:5).

Torah is the book of the past—recorded and sealed once for all. The prophets, and ultimately Messiah himself, spoke for the present. Theirs was a new word, but it was a familiar word drawn from the ancient book.

Righteousness, Righteousness You Shall Pursue

Parashat Shof'tim, Deuteronomy 16:18–21:9

Events in the United States over the past decade have left most people rather skeptical about the possibility of obtaining justice. Our legal system seems less concerned with righteous judgment than with providing a complex set of rules for a game that only a privileged few know how to play. Financial clout seems to count much more than the rightness of one's case. It may surprise us then to hear that one of the most impassioned phrases in Torah is about justice. In the midst of instructions on establishing a proper legal system, Moses cries out to Israel, *Tzedek tzedek tirdof* —"Justice, justice you shall pursue" (Deut. 16:20).

Tzedek, or justice, can also be translated as righteousness—the proper order of behavior, both public and private, that reflects the righteousness of God himself. Torah charged the judges of ancient Israel with establishing and maintaining righteousness among God's people, so that God would be honored. For emphasis and poetic impact, Moses repeats the word—*Tzedek tzedek tirdof.*

Since Torah is given by God, however, every word has its own weight and significance; none is wasted. If the word righteousness is repeated, it must be to emphasize two different aspects of righteousness. Ancient commentators said the word was repeated in this context to show that to pursue righteousness in general, one must pursue a righteous court.

We might add another interpretation; we are to pursue righteousness through our own deeds, and we are to pursue righteousness as a gift from God. Thus, Abraham believed the LORD and he counted it to him as righteousness (Gen. 15:6). This was a gift of righteousness that Abraham did not earn, but received from the

LORD. Likewise, earlier in Deuteronomy, the LORD commands Israel to circumcise their hearts (10:16), that is, to cultivate a right attitude that will produce righteous behavior; toward the end of the book (30:6), he promises that he himself will circumcise their hearts, that is, provide a gift of righteousness.

The prophets also speak of righteousness as a gift. Isaiah (in 53:11) writes of Messiah the suffering servant, who will bring this gift.

> He shall see the labor of his soul and be satisfied.
> By his knowledge my righteous servant shall make many
> righteous,
> For he shall bear their iniquities.

We are to pursue this gift of righteousness through trusting in God as a merciful and forgiving master. At the same time, we are to pursue righteous behavior on our own. Messianic believers sometimes feel that since they have received righteousness as a gift through the sacrifice of Messiah, their deeds, whether good or bad, do not matter. Some even act as if any real effort toward righteousness would somehow diminish the gift of righteousness. But Scripture indicates that we are to do both, to receive the gift through trusting in God, and to pursue righteousness in all we do.

During Rosh Hashanah and Yom Kippur, which come at the same time of year as this parasha, we seek both forms of righteousness. We consider our deeds, make amends, and resolve to change our ways as needed. On Yom Kippur we fast and confess our sins. And we also pursue the gift of righteousness that God originally provided for Israel through the scapegoat on Yom Kippur, and that he provides now through the sacrifice of Messiah.

Tzedek tzedek tirdof—righteousness, righteousness, you are to pursue. This brings us to the third word, "pursue." In the Western world, Justice is often portrayed as a blindfolded woman, holding a balance scale in one hand. She awaits those who will appeal to her, and decides their case impartially by objective laws. Thus, someone can admit misleading the public and withholding truth, but still claim to be just according to the technicalities of law.

The Hebrew view of righteousness goes beyond legal correctness to a deep instinct for what is right. It not only declares what is right; it pursues it. A poor man once came before his rabbi to ask if it was acceptable to recite Kiddush, the blessing for Shabbat, over a cup of milk instead of wine. The rabbi reached into his pocket and gave the man two hundred dollars, telling him to go buy all that he needed for Shabbat. When the rabbi's students asked him why he had done so, he said, "The man had no money for wine; that is why he was asking about milk." "Yes," said the students, "but why so much money?" "If he was planning to drink milk on Shabbat," replied the rabbi, "he also had no money for meat. I gave him enough to celebrate Shabbat properly with his family." This rabbi was not sitting as a detached judge, deciding on technicalities, but was pursuing righteousness.

We also are to pursue righteousness. "Pursue" is a strong and active word in the Hebrew, implying that we are not just to avoid obvious wrongdoing, but to positively address wrong and suffering as we are able. So, Moses instructs us:

> You shall not see your brother's ox or his sheep going astray, and hide yourself from them; you shall certainly bring them back to your brother. And if your brother is not near you, or if you do not know him, then you shall bring it to your own house, and it shall remain with you until your brother seeks it; then you shall restore it to him. You shall do the same with his donkey, and so shall you do with his garment; with any lost thing of your brother's, which he has lost and you have found, you shall do likewise; you must not hide yourself. You shall not see your brother's donkey or his ox fall down along the road, and hide yourself from them; you shall surely help him lift them up again. (Deut. 22:1–4, NKJV)

We are responsible for one another; righteousness means that we keep a look out for each other, and do what we can to help. We try to be fair, but we do not limit our behavior to what is fair. If we see those in our family, in our synagogue, or even out on the street, who are suffering, carrying a heavy burden, lost, or trying to find something that is lost, we are to come alongside to their aid. "You must not hide yourself."

Messiah himself provides the best example of pursuing righteousness. He is the righteous servant, and he makes many righteous. How? Isaiah said that he came among us, took on our sins, bore our iniquities. He is the great teacher, but he did not simply say, "If you are interested, come to me and I will teach you how to live." Instead, he saw us in need, and did not hide himself, but came to lift us up and return us to the Father.

Right Worship, Right Works

Parashat Ki Tetze, Deuteronomy 21:10–25:19

You shall not pervert justice due the stranger or the fatherless, nor take a widow's garment as a pledge. But you shall remember that you were a slave in Egypt, and Adonai your God redeemed you from there; therefore I command you to do this thing. When you reap your harvest in your field, and forget a sheaf in the field, you shall not go back to get it; it shall be for the stranger, the fatherless, and the widow, that Adonai your God may bless you in all the work of your hands. When you beat your olive trees, you shall not go over the boughs again; it shall be for the stranger, the fatherless, and the widow. When you gather the grapes of your vineyard, you shall not glean it afterward; it shall be for the stranger, the fatherless, and the widow. And you shall remember that you were a slave in the land of Egypt; therefore I command you to do this thing. (Deut. 24:17–22, NKJV).

Students of Torah have long noticed that Moses makes little distinction between what we might call ritual laws and ethical laws. This long middle section of Deuteronomy shifts, with no apparent design, from ordinances against idolatry to the regulation of warfare, from proper sacrifices to the inheritance rights of the firstborn. This discussion, as we read in the previous parasha, began with the words, *Tzedek tzedek tirdof*: "Righteousness, righteousness you shall pursue." The first word is repeated for emphasis, but the sages teach us that each word also has its own distinct meaning. Perhaps Torah repeats the word righteousness to show that we must be righteous toward God and righteous toward man. We must pursue right ritual and right ethics.

We might prefer to treat these two strands of righteousness separately. Torah, however, speaks of both strands in one breath, as in the command to provide justice for the stranger, the orphan, and the widow—the most vulnerable and disenfranchised elements within Israel. The rationale for this law is not only ethical, but also theological; we are to protect the disenfranchised because we were once disenfranchised ourselves in Egypt and Adonai our God redeemed us. Our treatment of the stranger, the orphan, and the widow reflects the holiness and character of the God of Israel. We remember his redemption by practicing redemption ourselves.

God himself enforces this linkage between his character and our behavior. Moses tells the Israelites that if they practice righteousness toward the needy, Adonai will "bless you in all the work of your hands." Conversely, Deuteronomy 15:7–11 warns Israel that if they oppress the poor man, he will "cry out to Adonai against you," and Adonai will hear. Likewise, "to your brother you may not charge interest, that Adonai your God may bless you in all to which you set your hand. . ." (23:20), and "You shall have a perfect and just weight, a perfect and just measure, that your days may be lengthened in the land which Adonai your God is giving you" (25:15). God steps into the midst of our "secular" concerns to show that, among the redeemed, there are no strictly "secular" concerns. All that we do reflects God's character, and God will reward behavior that reflects him accurately.

Messiah also taught that the two aspects of righteousness belong together. The "first and great commandment" is the Shema: "You shall love Adonai your God with all your heart, with all your soul, and with all your mind." The second commandment, Yeshua said, "is like it: 'You shall love your neighbor as yourself'" (Matt. 22:39). Why is this second command "like" the first? Because each is incomplete without the other. Love of neighbor is not only ethical behavior, but also an expression of love for God. Love of God cannot be expressed in ritual alone, but requires love of neighbor. Proper ritual without an ethical dimension is flawed. Religious observance that does not demand proper treatment of our fellow human beings, no matter how "spiritual" it may appear, will lead to self-righteousness, elitism, and irrelevance.

Jewish tradition recognizes this truth in its use of the word *tzedakah* (the feminine form of the noun *tzedek* or righteousness). Tzedakah, at least since the time of the Mishnah, refers to giving to the needy, to what we call in English "charity." As I learned as a child in Shabbat school, however, tzedakah involves more than charity. Rather, it is a religious obligation to help restore the ideal order among humanity, to recognize in action the inherent dignity of all human beings. Torah could have allowed the farmer to harvest his entire crop, and then practice charity by handing out a portion to the poor. Instead, it preserves the dignity of the stranger, orphan, and widow by granting them a share of the field. The gleanings belong to them. Further, Torah reminds the farmer that he was once vulnerable and poor as well. He must not take his current prosperity for granted, but recognize that it is a gift from God, to be shared with the community.

Such a teaching has vast social ramifications. We can begin to apply it, though, within the intimate society of our congregations. We are a redeemed people; our life together as a people should mirror that redemption. As in ancient Israel, there may still be unequal distribution of resources, but there is to be no oppressor among us, no one hoarding goods when others are in need. The resources of the congregation—the Scriptures, the public worship, whatever facilities it may possess—belong to all. Those who are powerful are to use their position to lift up those who are vulnerable.

In his New Covenant letter, Ya'akov reminds us that the redeemed community reflects this unique standard:

> For if a man comes into your synagogue with gold rings and fine apparel, and there also comes in a poor man in filthy clothes, and you pay attention to the one wearing the fine clothes and say to him, "You sit here in a good place," and say to the poor man, "You stand there," or, "Sit here at my footstool," have you not shown partiality among yourselves, and become judges with evil thoughts? Listen, my beloved brothers: Has God not chosen the poor of this world to be rich in faith and heirs of the kingdom that he promised to those who love him? (James 2:2–5)

The God we serve is concerned not only with proper ritual; he steps into the midst of our social arrangements to establish an order reflecting his redemption and justice. He demands that we not hoard his great act of redemption for ourselves, but disperse it among the needy.

Remember Your Roots

Now it shall be:
when you enter the land
that HaShem your God is giving you as an inheritance,
and you possess it and settle in it,
you are to take the premier-part of all the fruit of the soil
that you produce from your land that HaShem your God is
    giving you;
you are to put it in a basket
and are to go to the place that HaShem your God chooses to
    have his name dwell. . . .
Then the priest is to take the basket from your hand
and is to deposit it before the slaughter-site of HaShem your
    God.
And you are to speak up and say, before the presence of
    HaShem your God:
"An Aramean Astray my Ancestor. . ."
(Deut. 26:1–5, *Schocken Bible*)

The closing chapters of Torah look ahead to Israel's future. Soon the children of Israel will cross the Jordan into the Land of Promise. Moshe describes a ceremony that they are to follow when they harvest their first crops in the new land. They are to bring an offering of the first fruits to the priest and recount the story of their deliverance from Egypt, beginning with the Hebrew words *arami oved avi*. The ring of these three words in the original is memorable; the *Schocken Bible* seeks to capture their tone with, "An Aramean Astray my Ancestor." This phrase is clearly meant to be memorized as a lasting reminder to that generation, and the following generations, of their origin.

Once the children of Israel cease their wanderings, they are to remember their humble beginnings. The command to remember is a common enough strain throughout Deuteronomy. What is striking here, at this moment of great national triumph, is the reminder that our forefather Ya'akov was not only a wanderer, but a foreigner by descent. His land of origin was Paddan-Aram, to which he returned when it was time to seek a wife. He was not to marry a woman of Canaan, the land where, his father Yitzhak reminded him, "you are a sojourner" (Gen. 28:4). Instead he went to the house of his mother's brother, Laban the Aramean, and there sought a wife of his own lineage.

Thus, after offering their first fruits, Ya'akov's descendants are to remember, "my Ancestor was an Aramean Astray." Then they continue to tell the story: "And he went down into Egypt and sojourned there, few in number; and he became there a nation, great, mighty, and populous." Only in Egypt did we cease wandering and become a nation. And in Egypt we experienced oppression, bondage, and finally deliverance by the hand of the Lord.

Israel is not a just a racial entity; being a child of Israel is not a matter of bloodline alone. Torah does not share the preoccupation with race that is one of the curses of modern history. Instead, the farmer tells the priest, "I stand before you today not because of the purity of my pedigree, but because I have partaken of the story of the deliverance from Egypt. Today we have reached the climax of the deliverance, as I offer the first fruits of the Promised Land." When Israel took possession of its inheritance in a moment of national triumph, it was not to speak the language of national pride, but to recount the story of its simple beginnings.

The story recounted in the ritual of the offering of the first fruits became the heart of the Passover Haggadah. In the Haggadah, however, the opening words are interpreted differently, as, "An Aramean sought to destroy my father. . ." This is an ancient reading of the text that was favored by Rashi, even though it is less literal than "my father was a wandering Aramean." Perhaps it won favor over the more literal reading because it is difficult for us to think of our father as an Aramean instead of as a Hebrew, especially at Passover, our great national festival. Furthermore, this reading introduces the divine deliverance that is the heart of the Passover story. It reminds us that there have always been those who sought to destroy us: "Pharaoh decreed only against the males, but Laban sought to destroy all, as it is written, 'An Aramean sought to destroy my father . . . *arami oved avi.*'"

In our Parasha, on the other hand, the literal sense prevails because here we are speaking of God's choice of Israel. What sets Israel apart is not any sort of racial superiority; indeed, our ancestor was an Aramean astray. Instead it is the uniqueness of our story that sets us apart. God has chosen Israel as his segullah, his sealed and personal treasure, a treasured nation that he will set high above all the nations (Deut. 26:18–19). We are of the humblest origin, raised up only because God has drawn us into his story, but we have the most exalted calling of any nation.

Like the reminders of our humble origins, so the reminders of our great destiny are interwoven through the whole account of Torah. At Mount Sinai, the Lord tells us, "Now therefore, if you will obey my voice indeed, and keep my covenant, then you shall be a segullah to me above all people. For all the earth is mine and you shall be to me a kingdom of priests, and a holy nation" (Exod. 19:5–6). All peoples belong to the Lord and fall under his care. Israel, who shares its origin with all the peoples, he has separated as his own treasure to be a source of blessing to all the rest. Israel is the treasure, but it is a treasure assembled out of the common stuff of mankind.

Here we have one of the great tensions of Torah, and indeed of the whole life of the spirit. If we know the God of Israel, we are chosen, unique. But we are not chosen for ourselves. In the modern world, this idea of chosenness is considered a scandal. How can any religion or ethnic group seriously claim to be chosen above others? Has this not been the source of misunderstanding, oppression, and endless warfare down to our own day? Religious folk, Jews and Christians as well, have at times brought this accusation down upon themselves.

How often do we exalt the group instincts of pride and bigotry into some kind of divine calling? We know that we are chosen to be a blessing to the rest of humankind, but how often do we actually provide that blessing, especially to those who differ or disagree the most?

The ancient ceremony provides a lesson here. After bringing the basket of first fruits and recounting the story, the Israelite is to "set it down before the Lord your God, and worship before the Lord your God." The basket of first fruits is the tangible sign of being chosen by God, but it is to be set down before him. The real privilege, and the point of our story, is that those who began as wandering strangers now may draw near to worship the Lord God of Israel.

Beyond Repentance

Parashat Nitzavim, Deuteronomy 29:9–30:20

It is fitting that this parasha, which falls on the final Shabbat before Rosh Hashanah, contains one of the most extensive treatments of repentance in Torah. The word we translate into English as "repentance" is *t'shuvah*, which literally simply means "return." The Hebrew root, *shuv*, one of the more common verbs in Torah, indicates turning or returning in a variety of different senses, from bodily turning to deep inner restoration.

This verb appears seven times in the first ten verses of Deuteronomy 30. If we translate it consistently, we will gain fresh insight into the meaning of repentance.

> And it shall come to pass when all these things come upon you . . . and you shall RETURN your heart . . . and RETURN to Adonai and heed his voice . . . that Adonai will RETURN your captivity . . . and RETURN and gather you from all the nations where Adonai your God has scattered you. . . . And you shall RETURN and heed the voice of Adonai . . . and Adonai will RETURN to rejoicing over you . . . if you RETURN to Adonai your God with all your heart and with all your soul.

Here we see that repentance begins with a change of heart, an inward return to God and his word. This return must issue in a change of behavior, or else it is incomplete and ultimately meaningless. The penitent ceases going his own way and returns to the way of obedience. To such repentance, Moses tells us, God will respond by turning back to the one who is returning to him. The Talmud says, "If one comes to cleanse himself, he is helped [by God]" (Shabbat 104a). If a man returns to God, God will return to him. Thus repentance is not just a religious formality, but is a restoration of relationship, in which God and man both return toward each other.

Jewish tradition rightly emphasizes the centrality of repentance, especially during the Days of Awe from Rosh Hashanah to Yom Kippur. Indeed, these days are also known as the Days of T'shuvah, ten days in which to examine one's heart and one's deeds, to confess wrongdoing, make amends, and seek God's mercy before the arrival of the most holy day of Yom Kippur. Our parasha reassures the one who is practicing t'shuvah that God will indeed respond. In the words of the prophet, "'Return to me and I will return to you,' says the Lord of hosts" (Mal. 3:7).

It is not surprising, therefore, that we read this well-rounded picture of repentance just before Rosh Hashanah. What may surprise us, though, is that these ten verses intimate that repentance alone is not enough. In the midst of the seven instances of RETURN, the Lord promises to "circumcise your heart and the heart of your seed, to love the Lord your God with all your heart, and with all your soul, that you may live." Writing of this circumcision, Ibn Ezra notes that just as human hands remove the physical foreskin, so God himself will remove the spiritual impediment of the heart. If a man returns to God, God will return to him, and help him to sin no more.

Ramban sees this circumcision as a promise for the future, to be fulfilled in the final redemption at the coming of Messiah.

> In the days of the Messiah, people will naturally choose what is good. The heart will not desire what is improper and will have no craving whatever for it. This is the circumcision mentioned here, for lust and desire are the foreskin of the heart, and circumcision of the heart means that it will not covet or desire evil. Man will return at that time to what he was before the sin of Adam.

Just as physical circumcision, however, is more than simply removing a fleshly barrier, so circumcision of the heart is more than the removal of a spiritual impediment. Adonai will do even more than cleanse the penitent and remove the propensity to sin—he will bring him into a renewed covenant. When Moses speaks of the circumcision of heart, he is speaking to those who are already a covenant people, who are turning away from sin and back to covenant obedience. Now they will be brought into a renewed covenant that operates on a more profound level, just as circumcision of the heart is more profound than outward circumcision. They have repented, but beyond repentance there is transformation. This is the work of God through Messiah.

Circumcision of the heart, as Ramban points out later in his discussion, speaks of the renewed covenant that Jeremiah and Ezekiel describe. "This is the covenant that I will make with the house of Israel after those days, says Adonai: I will put my Torah in their minds and write it on their hearts; and I will be their God and they shall be My people" (Jer. 31:33). Likewise, the LORD says through the prophet Ezekiel (36:26): "I will give you a new heart and put a new spirit within you; I will take the heart of stone out of your flesh and give you a heart of flesh." This transformation is to take place in the days of Messiah.

A new circumcision means a renewed covenant, a covenant of the heart; yet there is more. Circumcision can only take place after a birth. Coming eight days after birth, it is in a sense a completion of the birth process. One full week passes, and then on the eighth day—day one of the new week—comes circumcision. Only then is the child given his name, because now the process of birth is complete. Could a circumcision of the heart imply a new birth?

Beyond repentance there is transformation, a transformation so thorough that it will render us new men and women. Torah calls us to return to its teachings and walk in its ways, but it also contains the promise of a renewed covenant and a new birth. It is up to us to repent, but God responds to our repentance. He seeks to make us into new people, so that we live not by our own ability to keep Torah, nor even by God's mercy when we fail. We live by the transforming power of a new life and a new heart. The God to whom we return is a God who transforms us.

Once a rabbi named Nakdimon came to speak with Yeshua the Messiah. Nakdimon has only spoken a few words when the master told him that he must be born again. Nakdimon marveled at this teaching, "How can these things be?" Yeshua's response is telling: "Are you the teacher of Israel, and do not know such things?" (John 3:9–10) If Nakdimon is a master of Torah, he must see that Torah points beyond itself to a God who will change us from within. Repentance is a return to Torah and its ways; beyond repentance is the new birth that Torah promises.

The Fear that Frees Us

Parashat Vayelekh, Deuteronomy 31

Jewish sovereignty in the land of Israel has been restored in our times, but many commandments of Torah must await the restoration of the temple and priesthood before they can be fulfilled. One such commandment is the law of *hak'hel*, the gathering to hear the Torah read in public once every seven years. In the days when the Temple stood, this gathering was to take place during the year of release. All Israel, men, women, and children, as well as the foreigners living in the Land, were to gather at the festival of Sukkot to hear the Torah. Every succeeding generation, Moses said, would "hear and learn to fear the Lord your God as long as you live in the Land which you cross the Jordan to possess" (Deut. 31:13, NKJV).

According to the Mishnah (Sotah 7:8), the king would read from a platform of wood set up in the courtyard of the temple. He did not read the entire Torah, but long passages from the book of Deuteronomy, concluding with the blessings and curses of chapter 27.

Since Israel's continuing presence in the Land was dependent on obedience to Torah, hak'hel was given to promote obedience and thereby safeguard that presence. Appropriately enough, when Ezra led the exiles of Israel from Babylon back to the Land, hak'hel appears to have been reinstated. In the year of Jerusalem's restoration, the people gathered as one in the open square before the Water Gate and asked Ezra to read the Torah in their hearing. Ezra read from morning until midday, standing on a wooden platform in the square, as his fellow scribes helped the people to understand the meaning of what they heard (Neh. 8:1–8).

Ezra varied from the strict letter of the law of hak'hel, however, because he began his reading not during Sukkot, but on Rosh

HaShanah, the first day of the seventh month. The people had just returned to the Land of Israel after seventy years of exile. Perhaps they were so eager to restore Torah to its central place, and to safeguard their presence in the Land, that they could not wait until Sukkot, the fifteenth day of the seventh month. Instead they began learning Torah as soon as the seventh month arrived.

In any event, the people's response to this reading is striking, and sheds light on one of the key concepts of Torah, the fear of the Lord. When Moses gave the instruction to read the Torah publicly every seven years, he told the Israelites twice to do so that they might learn to "fear the Lord." Clearly this was the goal of the public reading.

Today we often hear fear of God referred to in a negative way, as something that we outgrow as we develop a more mature spirituality than Moses had in mind. But in Ezra's day, when the people heard the words of Torah publicly expounded in the holy city, they did not have to stir up the fear of the Lord. It arose as a natural response: "For all the people wept when they heard the words of Torah" (Neh. 8:9). The fear of the Lord produced in them a sense of his holiness and their own unworthiness, and they grieved.

Such a response seems especially fitting when we remember that this was the first day of the seventh month, Rosh HaShanah, the beginning of the Days of Awe. The people mourned their own failure and inadequacy in the presence of the awe-inspiring God. The leaders, however, told them, "This day is holy to the Lord your God; do not mourn nor weep.. . . Do not sorrow, for the joy of the Lord is your strength" (Neh. 8:9–10). Why, at the beginning of the Days of Awe, when we are to examine our hearts and repent, did the leaders tell the people not to mourn, but to rejoice? Was it not fitting for them to mourn and weep as they heard the Torah and recognized the depth of their failure to carry it out?

The answer lies in the concept of the fear of God. The fear of God stirs us to obedience, to put God and his Torah first in our lives. It opens our eyes to our own shortcomings and indeed to our weakness and inadequacy before God. But let us not imagine it as a cringing, abject response. The fear of God does not paralyze us. No, David says, "The fear of the Lord is clean" (Ps. 19:10); it frees us from all other fears. It is significant that hak'hel, meant to instill the fear of God in Israel, took place in the year of release.

The Messiah taught the same truth about the fear of the Lord:

> Therefore do not fear them [your persecutors]. . . . Do not fear those who kill the body but cannot kill the soul. But rather fear him who is able to destroy both soul and body in Gehenna. Are not two sparrows sold for a copper coin? And not one of them falls to the ground apart from your Father's will. . . . Do not fear, therefore; you are of more value than many sparrows. (Matt. 10:26–31, NKJV)

The fear of God frees us from all other fears. If we are truly in awe of God during the Days of Awe, we will not be awed by any-thing else—even our own sins. The leaders told the people to re-joice because this was not a day to dwell on their shortcomings, but on God. "This day is holy to the Lord your God." The fear of God moved them to rely on his holiness and forgiveness alone.

During the Tashlich service on Rosh HaShanah, when we symbolically cast our sins into the depths of the sea, we recite Psalm 130:

> If you, Lord, should mark iniquities,
> O Lord, who could stand?
> But there is forgiveness with you,
> That you may be feared.

We moderns are often uncomfortable with the concept of the fear of God. We would rather imagine a totally accepting deity that would not stir up any negative emotions within us. But such a deity would be a man-made god, an idol. The fear of God frees us from such idolatry.

The God of Israel is a holy God who applies his own standard of holiness to those who would worship him. The fear of God frees us from the delusion that we can attain God's standard on our own. When we approach God and his Torah with the proper fear, we find the release and forgiveness that free us from fear. As we mark the Days of Awe, may we be like the people of Ezra's day who first "wept when they heard the words of Torah," and then "greatly rejoiced because they understood the words that were de-clared to them." (Neh. 8:9, 12)

The Rock that Follows Us

Parashat Ha'azinu, Deuteronomy 32

Great is this Song, for there is in it the present, the past, the future, and there is in it this world, and the World to Come. (Sifre Ha'azinu 333)

Torah contains two great songs composed by Moses. The first is the Song at the Sea, which Moses and the sons of Israel sang after the destruction of Pharaoh's army at the Red Sea. The second is this song that comes at the conclusion of the Moses's life, when Israel is about to enter the Promised Land. In both songs Moses the teacher, lawgiver, and judge, becomes Moses the poet and seer. Both songs arise at a defining moment in Israel's story. Indeed, the very term "Song" (*shirah*) in Torah implies a unique and transcendent statement.

The splitting of the Sea is the culmination of God's mighty acts of deliverance; a moment of great victory in which Israel leaves Egypt forever and the powers of the Egyptians are destroyed. "When Israel saw the great power that Adonai had used against the Egyptians, the people feared Adonai and they believed in Adonai and in his servant Moses. Then Moses and the children of Israel sang this song to Adonai . . ." (Exod. 14:31–15:1) At this moment Israel's bondage and humiliation are swept away and the vision of the Lord's greatness alone remains.

The song of Ha'azinu also comes at a decisive moment, but it is a moment that is filled with foreboding. Moses is about to die; he completes the writing of the Torah, and warns Israel that it will be a witness against them, because they are bound to rebel against it. This song is not a chant of victory. Rather, it opens with a call to the heavens and the earth to hear (*ha'azinu*) its words of testimony against Israel. As Sifre says, the song covers past, present, and future. Moses calls the heavens and the earth to bear witness because they also exist in past, present, and future. The song will speak to all generations of Israelites, from the one that first enters the Promised Land to the one that enters the age to come.

What then is the message of this Song? It reviews God's unchanging purpose for Israel in contrast with Israel's inconstancy. Then it reminds the people of the threat of exile about which Moses has already warned them, and concludes with the promise of final redemption.

> Rejoice, O nations, with his people;
> For he will avenge the blood of his servants,
> And will render vengeance on his adversaries,
> And will atone for his land and his people. (Deut. 32:43)

This long and tortuous history, however, is not the ultimate message of the Song. Its subject is not Israel, but the God of Israel, and in this Song Moses employs a distinctive word to describe him: the Rock. Israel wanders from God and must endure the trials of exile, but God remains constant, unchanging, and immovable. He is the same, past, present, and future, the Rock, as the Song reminds us several times (vss. 4, 15, 18, 30, 31).

This title for God survives in our liturgy. In the Jewish burial service today, the mourners recite verse four as the deceased is brought to the cemetery: "The Rock, his work is perfect, for all his paths are justice. A faithful God without iniquity, righteous and fair is he." The word "perfect" is *tamim*, meaning complete, whole, blameless. Just as the Song gathers the troubling and contrary events of Israel's story into one harmonious whole, so all God's work is a harmonious whole.

This truth is especially compelling as we face the loss of our loved ones. As burial puts them out of sight and out of reach, the present may make little sense. God's eternal purposes, however, remain. In the words of the siddur: "The Rock is perfect in every deed. Who can say to him, 'What have you done?' He rules below and above, brings death and brings life, brings down to the grave and raises up." In the Song, Israel faces failure and exile and is assured that God's good purpose transcends these; Israel will be redeemed in the end. Likewise, our burial service reminds us that God's good purpose transcends individual death and loss. He is the Rock; no circumstance can shake him—or those who trust in him.

"Rock" speaks of solidity, dependability, and unchanging purpose, but Torah reveals another aspect. It is from the rock that God provides water for the Israelites. The rock is a source of mercy and life. Hence, the Song speaks of the Rock of salvation (vs. 15) and the Rock "who gave you birth" (vs. 18).

In a striking blend of images, an old midrash says that the rock that provided water for the Israelites followed them throughout their wanderings.

> And so the well which was with the Israelites in the wilderness was a rock, the size of a large round vessel, surging and gurgling upward, as from the mouth of this little flask, rising with them into the mountains, and descending with them into the valleys. Wherever the Israelites would encamp, it made camp with them. (Tosefta Sukkot 3:11)

The rock that Moses struck to bring forth water (Exod. 17:5–7) has become a well supplying water to the Israelites every day. Just as God supplies the manna is every day, so he provides water. The Rock represents all that is steady and immovable, yet in God's merciful purposes, the Rock moves, to follow the children of Israel in all their wanderings. The unchanging Rock that spans past and future enters the present circumstances of the children of Israel.

Paul develops this midrash further in 1 Corinthians 10:4. "[Our fathers] all drank the same spiritual drink, for they were drinking from a spiritual rock which followed them, and the rock was Messiah." The mystery of Messiah is that he is the Rock, the eternal and unchanging One, and he is also present to every generation in need to supply the waters of life.

Significantly, the only other Song in the Torah, besides the two songs of Moses, is a song of the well:

> Spring up O well — sing to it! —
> The well that the princes dug,
> That the nobles of the people sank,
> With the scepter and with their staffs. (Num. 21:17–18)

Each of the three Songs of Torah unites past, present, and future in a harmonious vision of the divine purpose. Ramban sees the Song of Ha'azinu as a prophecy of the messianic age, an age that God institutes according to his mercy alone, whether we deserve it or not.

> In this song there is no condition of repentance or service of God as a prerequisite for the coming redemption, but it testifies that the evils will come and that we will endure them, and that he, blessed be he . . . will not destroy our memory. Rather, he will return and will punish our enemies.

Ramban sees this gracious promise as a fitting conclusion to the writings of Moses: "Certainly, we shall continue to believe and look forward with all our heart for the word of God by the mouth of his prophet [Moses]—peace be upon him!"

Simchat Torah

Parashat V'zot HaBrachah, Deuteronomy 33:1–34:12

The cycle of Torah readings nears its end, but the story seems to avoid a conclusion. It leaves us on the far side of the Jordan, not in the Land that has been Israel's destination since the Exodus from Egypt. Moses dies and is buried outside the Promised Land. Deuteronomy concludes in the plains of Moab, thus setting the stage for the crossing of the Jordan into the Land. Joshua succeeds Moses, and is filled with the Spirit just as he was, ready to lead Israel to the culmination of their journeys, the conquest of the Land. The scroll concludes, therefore, on a note not of mourning but of anticipation. It ends with the death of Moses, through whom we received Torah, but it ends on a note of hope.

Parashat V'zot HaBrachah, which contains these final scenes, is the only parasha not normally read on Shabbat. Rather, we save it for Simchat Torah, the holiday of rejoicing in the Torah, when we renew the annual cycle of readings. On Simchat Torah we reach the end of V'zot HaBrachah, only to begin again with Parashat B'resheet, "In the Beginning." The scroll reaches its end, but does not become a closed system. It preserves the lessons of the past, but leads boldly into the future, into a new cycle that is the same as, but somehow different from, the previous one.

Out of Torah's openness flows its unparalleled vitality. Every generation of Jewry has interpreted and reapplied the Torah, so that our entire walk through history as a people is rooted in it. In the Land of Israel, and throughout the Exile, we have had vast disagreements over specific meanings and applications, but Torah has served as the foundation for the Jewish dialogue everywhere. It is not only divine revelation, but the basis for an unending discussion of what has been revealed. If its story had ended with Israel's entry into the Land of Promise, it may have not followed us into Exile and served us there so well.

Furthermore, the Torah remains open because it points beyond itself. Just as its conclusion demands the entry into the Promised Land, so its final chapters abound in allusions to redemption in the more distant future. On the eve of Israel's entry into the Land, Moses warns of failure and exile, but also reassures Israel of their eventual return to God and the fulfillment of all his purposes for them. "And it shall come to pass, when all these things come upon you, the blessing and the curse that I have set before you . . . and you return to the Lord your God and obey his voice . . . that the Lord your God will bring you back from captivity . . ." (30:1–3). Torah seems not a finished and solid edifice as much as a vessel leaning into the future.

In one matter, however, the scroll does seem closed. After recounting the death of Moses, it reminds us, "Never again did there arise in Israel a prophet like Moses, whom Adonai knew face to face . . ." (34:10) Joshua is already established as his successor, yet he is not a prophet like Moses. What is the distinguishing difference? Adonai knew Moses "face to face," with the result that he performed unparalleled signs and wonders in Egypt and before the eyes of all Israel. This is the unique qualification of Moses, through whom the Torah was given. The Lord spoke to Moses, we are told (Exod. 33:11), "face to face, as a man speaks to his friend." The Lord angrily reminds Miriam and Aaron of this difference when they challenge their brother's authority (Num. 12:8). Moses' claim to authority is unique and unequaled; hence the revelation he received remains unequaled.

Maimonides refers to this aspect of Moses' stature in the seventh of his thirteen principles of the faith: "I believe with perfect faith that the prophecy of Moses our teacher was true, peace be upon him, and that he was father of the prophets, those who came before him and those who followed him." Or as the Yigdal prayer paraphrases the same principle: "There never arose in Israel another like Moses."

It would seem that here at least Torah is a closed book. That certainly was the intent of Maimonides and much of traditional Judaism. The Torah given by Moses is unique and irreplaceable because Moses was a unique prophet. He received revelation face to face, with an intensity and directness beyond that given to any other prophet. Hence, his book is like no other book and can never be superseded.

Yet even here Torah is a vessel leaning into the future. Before Moses' death, the Lord had already promised him, "A prophet like you will I raise up for Israel from among their brothers . . ." (18:15). The final words of Torah remind us that a prophet like Moses has not arisen. But such a prophet will arise: another one with whom God will speak face to face, who will perform great miracles, lead his people out of bondage, and institute a new covenant.

Followers of Yeshua recognize in him the prophet who is to come. He came from the very presence, or "face" of God, performed great miracles among his people, released multitudes from the bondage of disease, sin, and death, and instituted a new covenant for Israel. When Yeshua rode into Jerusalem for his final Passover, the crowds greeted him with waving palm branches and verses from the Hallel psalms, saying, "This is The Prophet, Yeshua from Nazareth in Galilee" (Matt. 21:11).

Such fulfillment, of course, lay many centuries in the future in Moses' time. The people were to await the prophet like Moses, but in the meantime, God would provide other leaders. Before Moses' death, the Lord had already commissioned Joshua with the words, CHAZAK V'EMATZ! "Be strong and courageous, for you shall bring the Children of Israel to the Land that I have sworn to them, and I shall be with you" (Deut. 31:23).

This charge, CHAZAK V'EMATZ, is repeated numerous times in the opening scene of the Book of Joshua. It becomes the rallying-cry of a new generation. Just as it takes strength and courage to uphold the legacy of the past, so it takes strength and courage to move forward into the future. Torah envisions this next step and prepares the way for it, even as it exalts Moses as the incomparable leader of the past.

On Simchat Torah we reach the end of the scroll and immediately return to the beginning to continue our reading for yet another year. At the conclusion of Deuteronomy, as with every book of Torah, we declare together, CHAZAK CHAZAK, V'NITCHAZEK! Be strong, be strong, and may we be strengthened! Torah is not a closed book, but a cycle; it ends not just with the death of Moses, but with the mandate for a new generation. The day of conclusion is the day of new beginnings.

Notes

Introduction

[1] Leonard Kravitz and Kerry M. Olitzky, eds. and trans. *Pirke Avot: A modern commentary on Jewish ethics* (New York: UAHC Press, 1993) p. 89.

[2] Carol Ochs and Kerry M. Olitzky, *Jewish Spiritual Guidance: Finding our way back to God* (San Francisco: Jossey-Bass, 1997) p. 122.

[3] Encyclopedia Judaica (Jerusalem: Keter Publishing House, 1996) Vol. 11, pp. 1507–1513.

[4] *Midrash Rabbah, Genesis, Volume One* (London, New York: The Soncino Press, 1983) p. xvi.

[5] *Midrash Rabbah, Numbers* (London, New York: The Soncino Press, 1983) p. 534.

[6] RASHI is the acronym for Rabbi Shlomo ben Isaac, born in Troyes, France in 1040. He also produced a definitive commentary on the Talmud, even as he made his living tending several vineyards that he owned. He lived through a period of mounting anti-Jewish persecution in France and Germany, especially in his later years, and died in 1105.

[7] Rabbi Moses ben Nachman, or Nachmanides, was born in Spain in 1195 and wrote extensively in many fields, including Torah. He participated in the most famous of the disputations that the Catholic Church forced upon medieval rabbis, the Barcelona disputation of 1263, after which Ramban found it prudent to leave Spain for Israel, where he died in 1270.

[8] "And Moses was not able to enter the tabernacle of meeting, because the cloud rested above it, and the glory of the LORD filled the tabernacle."

[9] R. Dr. Charles B. Chavel, trans., *Ramban, Commentary on the Torah, Leviticus* (New York: Shilo Publishing House, 1975) pp. 6-7.)

[10] R. Dr. Charles B. Chavel, trans., *Ramban, Commentary on the Torah, Exodus* (New York: Shilo Publishing House, 1975) p. 423.

[11] For a more systematic treatment of the weekly readings I recommend the Walk! series by my good friend Dr. Jeff Feinberg, being published by Lederer/Messianic Jewish Publishers. As of this writing, the first two books, *Walk Genesis!* and *Walk Exodus!*, are available.

The Book of Genesis

[1] The Schocken Bible: Volume 1. *The Five Books of Moses. A new translation with introductions, commentary, and notes by Everett Fox.* (New York: Schocken Books, 1995) pp. 3–4.

The Book of Numbers

[1] The Schocken Bible: Volume 1. *The Five Books of Moses. A new translation with introductions, commentary, and notes by Everett Fox.* (New York: Schocken Books, 1995) p. 650.

Bibliography

Alter, Judah Aryeh. Arthur Green, trans. *The Language of Truth: The Torah Commentary of the Sefat Emet.* New York: Jewish Publication Society, 1998.

Babylonian Talmud, Hebrew-English Edition. London: The Soncino Press, 1987.

Chavel, Dr. Charles B., trans. *Ramban: Commentary on the Torah.* Five Volumes. New York: Shilo Publishing House, 1975.

Herczeg, Rabbi Yisrael Isser Zvi, ed. *The Torah: With Rashi's Commentary Translated, Annotated, and Elucidated.* Brooklyn, N.Y.: Mesorah Publications, 1998.

Holy Bible, New King James Version. Nashville: Thomas Nelson Publications, 1994.

Kravitz, Leonard, and Kerry M. Olitzky, eds. *Pirke Avot: A Modern Commentary on Jewish Ethics.* New York: UAHC Press, 1993.

Kugel, James L. *The Bible as It Was.* Cambridge, London: Harvard University Press, 1997.

R. Nosson Scherman. *The Complete ArtScroll.* Brooklyn: Mesorah Publications, 1984.

Scherman, Rabbi Nosson., ed. *The Chumash, The Torah and Five Megillos with a commentary anthologized from the rabbinic writings.* Brooklyn: Mesorah Publications, 1998.

Freedman, Rabbi H., ed. *The Midrash Rabbah.* Ten Volumes. London and New York: The Soncino Press, 1983.

Neusner, Jacob. *The Mishnah: A New Translation.* New Haven and London: The Yale University Press, 1988.

Fox, Everett, trans. *The Five Books of Moses: Vol. 1.* New York: Schocken Books, 1995.